Mastering Your Own Spiritual Freedom

Lessons from *A Course in Miracles*

James Nussbaumer

Library of Congress Cataloging-in-Publication Data

Nussbaumer, James. – 1957

Mastering Your Own Spiritual Freedom by James Nussbaumer

This is the sequel to "The Master of Everything". This book is down-to-earth, accessible, illustrating his life and experiences behind prison walls. Readers will find an easy-to-follow path to healing of the separated mind: reaching illumination thus finding in their heart the free will that has been waiting for them, mastery accomplished. Hence the title: Mastering Your Own Spiritual Freedom.

1. Metaphysical 2. Manifestation 3. Co-Creation 4. Power of Thought

I. Nussbaumer, James 1957 II. Metaphysical III. Title

Library of Congress Catalog Card Number: 2016935199

ISBN: 9781940265353

Cover Design: noir33.com

Book set in: Calibri Light

Book Design: Tab Pillar

Published by:

PO Box 754

Huntsville, AR 72740

800-935-0045 or 479-738-2348 fax: 479-738-2448

WWW.OZARKMT.COM

Printed in the United States of America

To humanity for teaching me that *in quietness all things are answered, and every problem becomes resolved*

Table of Contents

Part IV: The Realization of Truth, Making No Room for Illusion

Part V: Knowing Who You Are

Part VI: The Answer to All That Imprisons You

Introduction

Some months after finding myself in prison for a foolish securities violation, a remorseful and shattered man, I was moved to a section housing "old" prisoners: anyone over thirty. There I discovered in my assigned footlocker a worn, musty, abandoned copy of *A Course in Miracles*—a book I had long been searching for to no avail. A miracle indeed! At that time, age fifty, removed from my high-pressured life as a financial advisor, I had the time to absorb the *Course's* complex lessons.

My studies revealed to me the nature of the prison in which virtually all of us dwell, that of the dominance of the ego and belief in separation from the One Mind (God). I also recognized the meaning of certain experiences I'd been having since my youth. I had found my work, and the direction I would take upon my release from prison. A voice or insistent thoughts told me what I needed to do. I began to write.

From there my first book, *The Master of Everything*, was born. The present volume is its companion—a sequel. Both are down-to-earth, accessible, and illustrated with stories and anecdotes from my life and experiences behind prison walls. But my purpose is to offer you an easy-to-follow path to the healing of the separated mind: illumination.

Almost immediately upon writing the final word of *The Master of Everything*, an urging came forward in my mind—that voice I mentioned—telling me there was yet much more I needed to write. I realized that another book, perhaps more, had just become my goal. Although I, myself, certainly felt complete, this recurrent voice was instructing me to extend what I had learned outward to others. With unmistakable clarity, deeper thoughts surfaced, telling me to "keep on writing." So needless to say, sometimes I need to be hit on the head and alerted twice, and here we are again.

Unfortunately for now, as I write this I am still in prison, my seventh year, with my ink pen flowing into the same type of black-and-white composition books in which I began what has become an exciting journey for me—with full faith that you, too, can begin opening your mind to look inside of it and find there is another way of looking at the world.

But first allow me to remind you where we have been in the previous book, and tell you where I am taking you now. For those who have read that first book but it has been a while, or for those who have not read it, it's important that I summarize and review its essential lessons so we can easily and comfortably move on from here.

In *The Master of Everything*, we discussed how to open yourself up so you may be guided to a supreme freedom of your own, through the deepest levels of forgiveness and a profound experience of miracles being part of your daily life. We realized that all things that frighten us occur in a world of illusion—that the world—a collective dream we call life—is merely a projection on a theater screen in our mind, which conceals a more real world.

A miracle is not a rearrangement of the figures in the dream of life, but an awakening from that dream. I'm not speaking of turning water into wine or parting a sea. I am speaking of seeking a practical goal as a whole: a return to inner peace. This does not mean trying to force something outside us to change via a miracle, but rather for something inside us to change. In other words, changing our minds on how we look at the world.

***

There's no doubt we all have had thoughts that at some deep level we're all related. I previously wrote about a more profound lesson: that if we go deeper yet into our minds we discover that we are not separate minds, but that we are actually the *same* mind. This is the concept of the "Christ-Mind." It is the idea that, at our innermost core, we are not just identical, but are actually the same being. We went on to learn that the "one begotten Son" does not mean only Jesus and not us—but rather that together we are the whole One Child of God.

I've used the word "Son" in both books as a genderless term representing the Oneness of "Christ" as a psychological term— our real consciousness. No religion holds a copyright on this one Truth. We learned that "Christ" is the whole Son of God, personalized, and refers to the common thread of divine love that has woven the innermost essence of the human mind.

Consider how a lamp with no electricity casts no light: nor does electricity without a lamp. Together, however, they cast out all darkness. This is the truth about us that is eternal—never changing—but we have forgotten it. Instead we identify with the notion of a small, separate self, and not the idea of reality, or Christ-consciousness, shared everywhere.

We learned how each generation looks to previous generations for lessons and recognized that this is why history repeats itself— absurdly. We continue to analyze the darkness in us in order to reach the light, and we only get more of the darkness because that's our focus. I will continue our discussion at greater lengths in this book that if we shine our light of truth onto the face of darkness, looking squarely at it and allowing it to draw closer to the light, the darkness fades away. Our inner light extinguishes darkness, and not the other way around.

We are not separate from God; nor are we separate from one another. We are the extended Thought of our Creator, where we are whole as genderless brothers/sisters in the family of God, called the Sonship. But mostly we choose to identify with duality;

we experience ourselves as the body instead of the "real" us. From that unreality—our identification with a body and its boundaries ruled by the separated mind, or ego—we form perceptions of the world based on time.

We learned that a separated consciousness—the ego-based mind—only thinks it has split away from the whole mind, sending us spinning into the dream of life here in this world. But this is where the Holy Spirit—a term for the real—intervenes. The Holy Spirit is the psychological aspect of our whole mind that heals the split, bringing it back to wholeness (or where we *think* we are being brought back, since we were never "not there"), where positive real thought can prevail and time is subdued. In other words, we experience the reality of light over darkness, or more simply yet—rising above adversity. But the ego continues to hound us with its own interpretation about our lives.

We took a look at how the ego-based mind uses guilt to make us fearful if we choose to go against the grain of the teachings of past generations. The efforts of the ego in all of us to reinforce our fears play out in a ridiculous yet powerful logic often responsible for many laws of our land. And we looked closely at the concept of sin as being unreal because it is of the separated mind that only dreams it is real. But we can circumvent the perceptions of the ego-based mind by sensing our true reality.

We considered how perception is not a bad thing; it's just not knowledge. I used the example of a rainbow, where you may perceive the colors and the number of colors slightly differently from my perception of it. How we perceive things brought me to a psychological interpretation of the Trinity: the One Mind of God, the Creator; the wholeness of Creation, or the Sonship; and the Holy Spirit that serves as our true light within, extinguishing darkness and guiding us to that wholeness. Thus the Trinity is our model for the whole-mind, unseparated.

***

A murder that I witnessed in an adjoining prison cell ultimately proved to me my own strength, due to my realization of our mind being naturally abstract, where death is not real. The mind's concentrated whole essence—the Oneness of God sustaining everything—has no separate parts that may die. We think we see death in the concreteness of separate identities, which we believe to be real. The ego in all its separateness cannot understand the abstract, so it only sees in the concrete. But with the Holy Spirit's healing we discover the difference between true reality and its opposite, the unreality of being split away from the wholeness of God.

In this book we will be going deeper into our source of conflict: how the ego's belief in separation makes us so fearful of death, veiling the truth of death's unreality and interfering with one-mindedness—which is God. We call this identification with the ego "wrong-mindedness."

The Holy Spirit of God—Who abides psychologically in a more positive-thinking side of the separated mind like an antivirus software installed in the hard drive of your computer—guides us out of separation and all its darkness. Since "He" is in the "right-minded" side, He is who we are. In *The Master of Everything*, we studied ways to identify with the "right mind" by shining our "spiritual flashlight"—invoking the Light of Truth, or Holy Spirit—on our fears and errors. In the present book, you are going to see through my own experiences the function of the Holy Spirit in His undoing of errors that leads to an awakened state and freedom from separate identities. I will be offering you exercises for use when your heart beats for a true purpose and the grip of the ego tries to hold you back. To begin *Mastering Your Own Spiritual Freedom* means to begin acknowledging the separated mind— the dream of form—and continuing your attempt to heal yourself. You will learn how to tap into your true essence: the Christ-Mind, which is the real divine "you."

You will begin realizing without fear the bridge the Holy Spirit has built for you from perception over to knowledge, where you will find that every individual you encounter becomes either a witness for the Christ in you, or for the ego in you. There is no middle ground. You will find it's okay to let the Holy Spirit reinterpret the world for you instead of relying on the ego's interpretation. Here is where you begin setting your goals, consciously opposite of the ego's goals.

Confidence cannot develop fully until mastery is accomplished. Hence the title: *Mastering Your Own Spiritual Freedom*. As you proceed through this book you will build confidence, knowing that your success in putting out darkness in your life grows by putting the ego behind you, and is guaranteed by God. In this alone you will inspire joy in others and may not even realize you are doing so. While you are here in a body, the ego will be with you, but you will have the power to render it a follower, manifesting only in unreal fussing, rather than what truly leads you. The ego's nonexistence can never truly match the Truth in you. I'll show you examples of how the Holy Spirit will not allow it, because you will have His shared inspiration.

You will learn to be more comfortable in knowing, not perceiving or guessing, that the body is merely a temporary structure projected by the separated mind, but is used as a communication device by the Holy Spirit. When the body's interpretation is left to the Holy Spirit rather than the ego, you will understand health as the natural state of everything that is real. You will understand sickness as illusion.

We're going to look into why we make idols, which are nothing more than a perceived anti-Christ-Mind, that help make the body seem to be valued more. An idol, you will come to find out, is a false impression, or a false belief that constitutes space between the Christ-Mind and what you think you see. An idol is nothing more than a wish or a dream, made only to seem tangible, given form, and only perceived to be real. You're going to realize why you will never be content with such illusion, and the real truth in why you must be careful what you wish for.

To master your own spiritual freedom you must discover that what stands beyond these dreams is your natural and real self which requires your whole mind to join with other minds; this is how peace is obtained. The willingness for peace is genuine here. But you must have genuine interpretations, too.

By sharing your interpretations with the Holy Spirit abiding in your right-mind, you sort out the false within you; and thus spiritual freedom is realized. Let's face it, we've all been weak at times, uncertain of our purpose, and unsure of what we wish for, where to look for it, and where to turn for help in our attempts. This can be terribly frustrating. But with Light comes clarity and peace. I invite you to use this book as a stepping stone onto that bridge from perception to knowledge, to cross over to the realization of your spiritual freedom the realm where we do not allow the world's illusion to become our illusions.

***

We are One; but your journey will be your own. Initiating peace will come forward in a form each mind seeks out of honesty and can understand. My true story of the efforts of a seventy-eight-year-old man to get out of prison safely and return home to his two sons will prove that we are all entitled to miracles. When our readiness is sincere, whatever form this lesson takes will be planned for us in such a way that we cannot mistake it. However, if there is no real sincerity involved, this only means there is no Divine plan for this form. The ground will not be prepared because no groundwork is needed for insincerity. In other words, in the absence of a true desire, false ideas will pop up as illusion spreads.

To begin now in bringing on your journey to spiritual freedom, you must be willing to recognize it as a true desire, and then the groundwork will begin being laid out for you. You must deeply want this to happen, or nothing will result. Like I already said, there is no middle ground. This can be no idle wish or fanciful dream. No aligning yourself with particular stars or planets will help. There is no magic or mystical formula, no compromise or bargain involved. To be sincere means that you acknowledge illusions for the false ideas they are, and are requesting *the real* in place of these bargained-for dreams.

This is not one of those books asking you to pray for long hours or make special sacrifices. But you do need to start searching your mind carefully to find the *free will* that is waiting for you. It has already arrived in your heart, but you need to *notice* it and accept it. Ask yourself, "What is truly in my heart?"

Forget any avenues the world directs you to take or the tidbits given by well-meaning but misinformed family and friends. Consider what you *know* will comfort you and bring peace to you, as well as to others. Don't allow some desires to be more acceptable to you than others. They all need to be seen as one mission, sharing the same amount of sincerity. All you need to do is ask yourself if you feel compromise slipping in between decisions to be made. You can easily do this by asking yourself two simple questions: *"Is this what I would have for my true free will?"* and *"Is this what will truly give me the peace of God?"*

Your answers will guide the choice you make. Don't be deceived that it should be otherwise, or that you are acting selfishly, because as you will learn in the pages ahead, you are merely "bringing it all to Him." There are no compromises, and your choice needs you to be operating your life freely. You are going to discover that choosing Divine Peace is choosing your free will; otherwise you choose illusory situations and circumstances that will lead to grief and frustration. Don't get me wrong—if you go along with illusion you may attain some wonderful things, it will seem, at least for a time. But aligning yourself with illusion will not bring you peace.

Your true desire is not a dream. We must constantly ask ourselves, with deep sincerity, what it is we truly want, and then listen for the answer, or an "urging" or "voice," if you will. Otherwise we end up reaching for what others really want, and put our efforts into what they advise is best for us. I know, because I did this myself for most of my adult life—but not any longer.

My goal in writing this book started with a picture of you—you wanting peace, wanting spiritual freedom, wanting to see how I have turned things around for myself so you can do the same. I can assure you that no one who truly searches for the peace of his or her own true free will can fail to bring it out of himself or herself, because it has always been within you. So let's get started by posing to yourself a simple question: How can you remain unsatisfied, when you ask for what you already have?

PART I

THE PATH TO FREEDOM

Chapter 1

A Bite of Life

Eve returns home from a long day and decides to freshen up a bit while she waits for Adam's return from his day in the jungle. Humming, she showers and primps while she listens for his step. He's home! As he walks in the door he grabs an apple from the fruit bowl on the kitchen counter. Eve had gone outside early in the morning and picked the fruit off the tree in the backyard.

Adam heads straight to the sofa, tired but content. There's much he wishes to tell her this evening, he says. As he removes his shoes, he yawns and stretches, then kicks his feet up onto the coffee table. While he bites into the apple, Eve steps quickly to the kitchen for some wine. She brings two wine glasses and the bottle back to Adam for him to open. She knows he likes to remove the cork himself.

She smiles with satisfaction. Adam is wearing the shirt she picked out for him as a special gift two months ago. She loves the mischievous air it lends him. He takes life so seriously. Eve loves these times, when he's relaxed and lets himself go in conversation. Eve doesn't find the subject he's telling her about particularly interesting, but at least he's talking and opening up to her.

While he chatters, she advances toward the sofa, feeling lustful and sensual. She has a spontaneous urge to kiss him and interrupt his chatter, just to celebrate the moment. For once she feels in charge and decides to initiate foreplay, instead of his doing it all the time—a responsibility he complains about bitterly. Now is her chance to surprise him.

She knows Adam is watching her from the corner of his eye. He smiles as he takes the wine glasses and sets them on the table. He responds to her first kiss with visible pleasure. But the more she insists on going further, the worse it gets. She feels his whole body stiffening, as if refusing any further involvement. He's still smiling, but his face is frozen. He has stopped talking and reaches for his wine.

Eve knows that Adam is uneasy; she can't seem to figure him out. But she thinks she can try, and she doesn't like what she's beginning to pick up on. The truth is that when she initiates foreplay, it never goes very far. It's never the right time, and he often says he's too tired or too busy or has a headache. Eve thinks he is behaving like a fearful little boy. She'd love to send him back to his childhood, all wrapped up and labeled "Damaged Goods."

***

From Adam's point of view, though, the picture looks different. Eve had already been home for a while before him, and as he walked in the door, her scent was in the air, blending with the fragrance of the garden the early evening breeze sends through the open windows. The sound of ducks splashing and quacking on the lake beyond their house adds a musical note, and the view is almost as lovely as Eve is looking. She asks him with a sensual tone in her voice if he'd like some wine, and of course he accepts. He loves it when she's in a good mood and caters to his every need and whim. At times like these, life is beautiful. He feels lucky to be pampered in so many ways; it makes him feel special.

While Eve goes into the kitchen, Adam continues to talk about anything and everything, just to make her laugh, because he knows she likes him to tell her about his day. As he is talking, he suddenly feels the urge to make love to her. If only she'd make the first move, he thinks, which she hardly ever does, then he'd be in seventh heaven. And what luck! There she is, offering herself to him, and fantasy has now become reality.

But something's wrong. Such forward passion makes him feel shy and upsets him. *It's as if her life depended on it, as if any man could satisfy her now*, he thinks. His confusion begins to haunt him. It's true he had told her that he wishes she would take the initiative now and then; but when she does, he realizes he feels alarmed. The truth is, he likes to be the aggressor; he needs to feel in control.

She has set her glass on the table and presses against him, kissing him. Now she is begging him to say "I love you." He thinks sarcastically to himself that maybe he should make a recorded message so she can listen to it all day long. The situation is getting on his nerves. Is it sex she wants, or love? He can't help but ask himself: Where does this need for affection come from? It must be a need so great that he dare not get too close for fear of being manipulated. A thought quickly arises; one he's had before: Did she have other lovers? Was she like this with them?

After about the sixth kiss, he stretches out an arm to get his glass of wine. He hopes his uneasiness has gone unnoticed, but knowing her intuition, he can never be sure. He considers "accidentally" spilling his wine on the rug. But on second thought, he decides to go to the bathroom to compose himself and stall for some time, hoping for a new attitude—his or hers.

***

As Adam heads into the bathroom, Eve recognizes, disappointed, that Adam is running away again. But this time she won't run after him. She's had enough. Enough of this male indifference, this rejection. Enough of acting like a nice girl. Enough of making his favorite meals and fulfilling his bedroom fantasies in exchange for the affection never given. Eve's anger begins to mount, and she resolves to give him the silent treatment. What she wishes to say seems too awful, too vicious. For now she'll hold it inside. Five minutes ago she wanted to kiss him, but now she wishes to get even. *Just wait till he comes out of the bathroom.*

***

Holed up in the bathroom, Adam reproaches himself. *After all, she did all that to please me.* If he followed her initiative for once, if he'd simply give her the love she expects, it would end the petty war they keep replaying. Why not tell her he loves her and lead her into the bedroom? So he returns to the living room full of good intentions.

He finds Eve distant, cold, and snappy, curled up in a ball at one end of the sofa. Dr. Jekyll has been replaced by Mrs. Hyde. His amorous intentions instantly dissolve. *If it's war she wants, then that's what she'll get*, he thinks to himself. He won't be manipulated like this! Ever since she's been visiting that snake of a therapist and begun to assert herself, it seems the problems have only increased.

Then she starts one of her tirades on commitment. Adam's blood curdles. He swallows a gulp of wine to calm down, but it tastes like vinegar. In a flash, he seems to have grasped the heart of the problem. She's an inconsiderate, jealous little brat, insane! Everything she touches she tries to dominate. Another ruined evening, and he has only one thought in mind, which is to leave. He tries to interrupt her accusations and name-calling so she can hear his decision, but she takes the words right out of his mouth.

"I suppose you want to leave again. Perhaps you think I'm disturbed, don't you? But isn't it really that I am disturbing to you? A pain in your rear? Do you honestly think other women are different? Do you really think you'll ever find the ideal woman? Look at yourself—you are pathetic!"

The Dance of Blame

What I've just described is a conflict over who is right and who is wrong. This is how it seems to go, on and on, again and again: the dance of blame and accusations. The tone will escalate; doors will slam. Somebody will leave and return. There will be a few screams, a few tears, bitterness on both sides, contrition, a little kiss or a peck, and on a good night, make-up sex. In a few days it will start all over again. Does this sound familiar?

You're probably thinking that this only happens to you and a few others you hang around with. But it happens everywhere around the world, and not only in intimate relationships. Of course, you will add your personal touch, as I have always done. In some cases people resort to physical violence to go along with the verbal and emotional violence. But in general the scenario does not vary all that much. Sometimes you would think that human relationships follow a predetermined program that is passed on for each generation to follow.

She says that she's ready for a man who is capable of commitment. She wants him to give her what her father never could. But the fear of such expectation is too much, particularly because he has no idea what intimacy really is, either with others or himself. He understands power, fame, mechanics, and bright ideas. But emotions are something else. He lacks the main ingredient in the love recipe, the ingredient she claims to have herself. As a result, he feels worthless at the emotional level.

He feels guilty for not responding to her lifelong dream and knows he cannot adequately fit the expected role. She's unhappy for not being able to make him happy, no matter how much she tries to help him become the Prince Charming of her dreams. He feels controlled, manipulated, forced into being what he is not. He felt the same confusion around his own mother, who also tried to turn him into a prince. It's a replay of the same dream. She has the grip on him without realizing it. She doesn't realize what a burden her dream is.

Likewise, he has no idea of the weight of his demands on her, nor his negligence. He is not aware of his behavior being the price he makes her pay for her dream. This is how he manipulates her, making her try so hard to reach him. This is how it slowly becomes unbearable. For her, it's as though she waits for him and follows him. And he, when she does, maintains his silence and runs away.

All their actions betray what they hope to obtain from each other, and both are deceived. They keep up the same game anyway. Some do so maliciously, to see how far the other will go before giving up the dream. Others go on out of helplessness, and when they have had enough of the maneuvers, when they have sufficiently trampled each other and have used up their entire arsenal, they will break up in disgust.

She will say that she has once more been taken for a ride and was abused. He will say he's once again fallen into the same old trap. Both will suffer because it didn't work out. She will most likely be awarded the only remaining chandelier left hanging and will consider herself to be the victor. He will say, "Good riddance."

For centuries, friends, lovers, families, nations, and even religions have danced to this broken record of conflict. But isn't it true that since time began, a major crisis might make us consider changing the music? But do we?

Chapter 2

The Real World

Try now to take a quiet moment; and in your mind's eye, see yourself facing a crisis. With that crisis, do you change? Let's say it's the death of someone dear. Picture yourself going to the funeral. The sky is cloudy, dark, and gray as you drive to the funeral parlor or church and park your car. Inside you notice beautifully arranged flowers; soft organ music is playing. You recognize the faces of family and friends as you find your way through the room. You feel the shared sorrow of loss, as well as the joy of having known the individual that radiates from the hearts of the people present. You sense a certain oneness, a unified purpose for being there with others.

As you walk to the front of the room and look inside the casket, you suddenly come face to face with yourself. This is your funeral, a few years from today. All these people have come to honor your life, to express feelings of love and appreciation for your contribution to their life.

As you take a seat and wait for the service to begin, you look at the program in your hand. There are to be four speakers. The first is from your family, immediate and also extended: children and others who have come from all over the country to attend. The second speaker is one of your friends. You've played a lot of golf with this guy over the years; his goal is to give a sense of what you are to the core as a person. The third speaker is from your work or profession. The fourth is from your church or some community organization, where you volunteered your service.

Now think deeply and sincerely. What would you like each of these speakers to say about you and your life? What kind of husband or wife, father or mother would you like their words to describe as a reflection of your presence in their lives? What kind of son or daughter? What kind of friend? What kind of work associate?

What character would you like them to see in you? What contributions or achievements would you like them to remember? Look carefully at the people around you. What difference would you like to have made in their lives? Try to honestly find these answers within yourself.

Once you have looked at this picture and found the answers, you have touched for a moment—glimpsed, however briefly—much of the real, deep, fundamental, and natural aspects of your mind: the value of who you are. You have, in that brief instant, established contact with that Inner Guidance system at the core of your true essence. This is the center of the Light that is *what* you are. It's your Divinity. In other words, this communication was with your real self, your own holiness. Or we might simply say: It is your spirituality.

You were briefly in a *timeless zone* that is the *real world*, until quickly a false idea of who you are—called the ego—crept back in and convinced you that *time* is your reality. The ego is not a friend of time, but pretends it is; it uses time in order to convince you of separateness instead of wholeness.

The ego-based mind uses time to keep you loyal by keeping conflict alive because it wants "you"—the real you—to be part of its thought system that believes it "makes its own reality." Sound familiar?

The ego-based mind supplies our thoughts of conflict, our questions and doubts about life beyond this world, and our worries about the future. Without time, nothing can cause conflict. There is nothing to try to make sense of without time, nothing to be curious about, and nothing to strive for. As we move along I will address why the ego-based mind is the preferred thought system from which most of us operate, though we don't realize it. We'll also examine another option: the timeless.

The ego in all of us has its creed to live by: "Gain at all cost." It does not trust death because it's afraid, not knowing what to expect. Therefore, the ego's strange religion must teach itself, and you, that it can promise you a future beyond the grave— complete with its own uncertain ideas of Heaven. It tells you that your unwillingness to buy into its teachings can result in an eternal future burning in a place of its own invention, Hell. This is the ego's primary scare tactic, and it religiously uses this concept for its survival. The ego speaks to you of Heaven, but insists you are not ready and that more preparation is needed. But let me ask you a question, and then I'll help you answer it. If the ego teaches you these things, these false ideas of yourself and of the world, then who teaches the ego? You do, and this is why it makes a life for you based on these false ideas that seem to be a vicious circle. The ego creates the circle of illusion, a path to nothing.

Chapter 3

Getting on the Path

Ever since the symbolic Garden of Eden, humanity has clamored for freedom. The quest to find the path to freedom seems to be man's purpose, regardless of race, era, nationality, or geography. But in spite of the fact that freedom has been sought for millennia, few individuals or nations really have knowledge of the road to take. Different people choose different paths for different freedoms, and for different values. These paths are usually traveled with limited goals and can often find themselves in conflict with the rest of the world, thus causing problems.

We then seem to treat the symptoms that arise without really treating the problem. For example, world leaders continue to stockpile weapons of mass destruction with the ever-present threat of using them against each other. We can argue with other nations about this problem until we're blue in the face, and these destructive devices will continue to be built. Why? Because we don't have the knowledge of how to get rid of the doubts and fears and thoughts of lack, that is causing hatred in our hearts. If we can't solve this, generations to follow will carry within them the same false will to continue planting the same seeds of hatred which we continue to pass down to them, and ultimately will manufacture a mechanism more powerful than any nuclear weapon we can imagine. Certainly we see a lack of freedom here.

Relative freedom—the usual type people strive for—is related to the type of existence people wish to lead. For instance, those who identify themselves with their country or nationality instinctively work for national or political freedom. Those who are motivated by economic goals strive for the power of money, which they view as financial freedom. Those who are inspired by religion work toward religious freedom. Those who possess some sociological or cultural beliefs promote freedom of assembly or freedom of speech.

These ideas of freedom, which grow from limited goals, are illusory and cause separateness and division in the world. Some other person or group must lose in order for others to gain.

I'd like to share a parable I've carried around in my mind for many years that has kept me inspired, and recently has taken on a new meaning for me and my life ahead.

> A beggar had been sitting by the side of the same road at the same time every day for over thirty years. One day a stranger walked by.
>
> "Spare some change?" mumbled the pauper, while holding out his old Cleveland Indians baseball cap.
>
> "I have nothing to give you," said the stranger. Then he asked, "What's that you're sitting on?"
>
> "Nothing," replied the beggar. "Just an old beat-up crate I have been sitting on for as long as I can remember."
>
> So the stranger asked, "Ever looked inside?"
>
> "No," said the beggar. "What's the point? There's nothing in this ugly box."
>
> "Have a look," insisted the stranger.
>
> The poor man managed to pry open the lid. With astonishment, disbelief, and elation, he saw that the box was filled with gold.

We are all sitting on such a box; in fact, we *are* the box. By holding this book in your hands, you are telling yourself that you have the desire to find out more, even if it means looking deep inside yourself. Regardless of the material possessions that bind you to good or bad, spiritual freedom is always your bottomless box of gold. This is true because our inherent spiritual freedom is our true essence. It's what we are; it is eternal, infinite, and changeless. When conditions "out there" for a free life are completely fulfilled and guaranteed, our mind will still be imprisoned if we fail to find spiritual freedom first, before any other.

Sometimes people think that calling on God is being spiritual — that inviting an outside force to our lives will make everything rosy. But the real truth is that we must invite everything that's already within us to grow, and growth can be messy — as I've discovered. The purpose of life is to grow into our own perfection. Once we open up to God, everything that could anger us is on its way out. This is so because the place where we go in anger is behind the ego-wall we have built, instead of love. We may not be able to walk through this wall, but we can learn to walk around it. Any situation that needs healing needs our love, and is where we don't yet have the capacity to be unconditionally loving. Without this we spontaneously fall back on doubt and fear.

It is the function of our Guided Thought deep within to draw our attention to this condition, by helping us more and more to move beyond that point of anger by His undoing of our errors. Without doubt, fear vanishes, leaving room for love. What is this gift we've all been given to free us from this illusion? It's the One Thought of unconscious intelligence, which is the Spirit of God, or the Spirit of our Divinity. This Divine Spirit is called by many "the Holy Spirit." But you can call it George, or Alice, or whatever you like. Religions hold no copyright or patent on this word or its interpretation.

What I am calling the Holy Spirit, the communicating aspect of God, revolutionizes in a *psychological* sense our understanding of why we are here on Earth, rather than addressing religiously why we exist. In this psychological manner, the Holy Spirit's means for undoing entanglements are evident everywhere. This Spirit, which is of the One Thought that created who we truly are, abides in our unconscious, and consciously brings about our purpose. We, in turn, are the learning link of the One Thought that teaches us love as our only purpose.

Everything we do is interpreted by either our self-made ego or the Holy Spirit. The ego leads us further into anxiety by using our body against another for physical gain. The Holy Spirit aspect of our mind uses everything to lead us to inner peace, giving us the physical means necessary for our ultimate purpose. The ego religiously uses time to live and die. The Holy Spirit psychologically and physically uses time to untangle illusory thinking and to direct us along the path to our free will.

The wealth we maintain within us lacks nothing, but the ego urges us to continually look outside, where the world of illusion promises more. Anything not of the One Thought of God must be illusion and is unreal. Why is this? Whatever is not true must be false, wouldn't you agree? Only truth is real and unalterable. What is real is all that we need for life eternal, and it's not located "out there" in any type of special place. Your truth is within you.

Have you ever had that gut feeling about an issue that concerned you, only to go with that feeling, thus resolving the matter? Sure you have. But that truthful "gut feeling" came from within you and not from a cloud in the sky. It was given to you from that One Thought of Truth within you, the Holy Spirit as the communicator, creating a bridge from your "gut" perception over to knowledge. Let's face it: we always have perceptions, but there are times when we bypass perceiving something first and simply *know* it to be truth.

Finding the Link

Any type of freedom we see as external—political, social, financial—is restricted by our contact with other individuals. These types of freedom are subject to being redefined or restricted by the limits imposed by man's laws. We then start to have state or national rights subjected to judiciary or violent readjustments, due to overlapping "rights" of other states or nations. The constant adjustment of these so-called controlling interests becomes a bondage, rather than freedom.

Only spiritual freedom is absolute and unlimited. By understanding this, the Holy Spirit automatically and unwittingly brings about a readjustment of material surroundings, and we will find ourselves with everything we need, including peace. Does He do this task with some sort of magic? Miracles are the only method, and are accomplished through the use of ongoing change, which requires the help of time. Intolerance, pride, and selfishness are shed, and everything takes on a new, enlightened meaning, thus allowing the relative freedoms to truly be free, and enjoyed.

How do you link yourself to this One Thought and gain spiritual freedom? By looking inside yourself and acknowledging that truth was never born and will never die; because you are truth—you are this intelligence brought forward from the unconscious to the conscious. Although you are one with all of eternity, the ego constantly will interfere with you consciously, and these are the entanglements that the Holy Spirit will undo.

Rather than stressing the limitations of some individuals in achieving this Oneness, the emphasis should be placed on the limitation of all individuals, because we're all in this together. Rather than stressing the need that "I" help "you" or "you" help "me," it must be "we" helping "us." Rather than making ourselves and others helpless-minded, we must become helpful-minded spiritually, and must help others to become so as well, without thought of personal gain.

What might this condition look like? A man stepped aboard a train one day, and one of his shoes slipped off and landed on the track. There was no time for him to retrieve it as the train began to move. To the amazement of his companions, the man calmly took off his remaining shoe and threw it onto the tracks. When asked why he gave up his remaining shoe as well, the man replied, "The man who finds both shoes lying on the track will now have a pair he can use, which may give him a better day."

When we identify with the ego, we think only of ourselves, like a man clinging to a single useless shoe, lamenting our lack and profoundly out of balance. When we are helpful-minded, we are focused on how others might benefit from our actions and we are at peace. This is spiritual freedom. Any other, lesser form of freedom is like a house built on sand. There is no greater gift than that of spiritual freedom, and no task more important than helping others achieve it.

An individual who mistakenly believes he is lost or lacking may live a lifetime of misery in the ego's domain, where all of his actions are shaped by this illusory picture. But if some event in his life challenges him so deeply that he unthinkingly steps forth with great courage, then the illusion will suddenly vanish, and he will see himself as a different being. Often it takes a real crisis to bring out a sure knowledge of the real inner self, and it's always a creative true free will.

Truly happy people are rare; too often the smiles we see are a brave front of the ego, a false idea of one's self, to mask varying degrees of internal misery. Yet everywhere, and in every walk of life, people are seeking happiness and searching desperately for a means to break out of the trap their lives have become.

If you feel bound and imprisoned, by asking the Holy Spirit for guidance you can be released from this trap. This asking constitutes your spiritual birth, and then you can travel along the path of spiritual freedom. In the pages ahead, my goal is to help you discover the same answers that I have. These answers, I am certain, will help you to obtain real vision and keep you alert along your spiritual journey.

Chapter 4

Your Abstract Way

You and I are touring an art gallery in Venice, Italy, and our eyes are glued to a thirteenth-century tapestry. The sign at the exhibit tells us the tapestry depicts Adam and Eve's expulsion from the Garden of Eden, and that the name of the artist was lost centuries ago. We both agree this work of art is a mind-opening portrayal of the garden paradise.

In the tapestry, overlooking Adam and Eve, you may see a wise old owl sitting on the end of a tree limb. But I may see the tree limb as God's arm and pointing hand, directing the couple to exit the garden. Additionally, I seem to see a monkey following the couple with his tail in the air, possibly saying "I told you so." But you see this area of the image as an angel guarding the Tree of Knowledge. Regardless of the specific images our eyes identify, we share the same experience of awe at the story's meaning. In *The Master of Everything*, I describe in detail my own take on the symbolism in this tapestry; it's a wonderful example of how, due to concrete thinking, we "lose ourselves in this world."

The ego has no problem telling us that before our birth we were with God in Heaven. There are also fairy tales, poems, and songs written about this. The ego will go on to teach us that life is painful and that we must sacrifice in order to return to Heaven, or the alternative will be "hell to pay" later. But what the ego cannot or will not even try to remember is that *it made itself* when the mind decided to dream of better ways, separate and apart from the One Thought of God. The ego cannot remember ever making the decision to separate because it still dreams. In fact, that's all the ego is capable of. It will only believe what has been passed down by previous generations, and these many beliefs are as solid as concrete. At least it thinks so, therefore continues to believe that it will find finer things within its own separate thought system.

Being that the ego is manmade and finite, its output is nothingness: illusion. It ends with the death of its body. Without the body it cannot exist. The ego idolizes bodies, even for Divinity purposes, and wishes its own to be more than what it is. But illusion is the best it can produce, and producing is always its goal until "nothing" can be better. We get stressed out over nothing, angered, and have attack-type thoughts, due to the ego's feeling of lack. These ego illusions seem to be quite specific. Why?

Our whole mind is naturally abstract, meaning that it is not practical, and is thus hard to understand by the practical. When I speak of the mind, please don't picture the brain, which is of the body. The mind causes the brain to function through the part of the mind that sees itself as separate from God. The abstractness of the whole mind is a concentrated essence keeping it one, or whole. The ego resists this abstract oneness; it dreams about occupying a small part of the mind as separate. This is the part of all of us that can only think in concrete terms. It is split off, or separated from, the naturally abstract. The image of Adam and Eve departing from Paradise is a symbolic representation of the splitting-off of the ego from the Oneness of God: the separation. The unknown thirteenth-century artist portrayed what he naturally was aware of through the wholeness of his essence. To him, what he envisioned as real could not be explained or portrayed in the concrete. Look at it this way: The concrete part of us believes what it wishes to be true, like those thoughts of lack, doubt, and fear I mentioned earlier, because it has constructed itself to be concrete. In other words, concrete is hard as rock but can be split apart. The ego must depend on the concrete because that is all it can understand, being hard as rock, and it needs to feel concrete to believe in its own survival.

Our mind has two separate thought systems: the real and the unreal. The real is of the abstract, and it is all that it has ever been and ever will be. The real never dies. The other is based on the body's birth, sickness, and death, with survival methods in between. This "in-between" part is its focus. This latter thought system is the ego, which is fearful of anything that is not concrete, including God. The ego loves to put the "fear of God" into its idolizing and calls it worship. It asks that we become "God-fearing" individuals in order to improve our well-being, and it teaches that good is never good enough.

The ego perceives everything as a separate whole, including other people. The ego is against communication except for its use in furthering separateness. It continues to build its own communication system based on its need to receive and survive. Its only concern is to protect itself, and it has no need otherwise to communicate. The ego will fight to the bitter end to defend its ideas and its own separateness when it feels threatened. This is why its way is to stockpile the most bombs. The ego is not evil, nor is it the devil—although the ego will quite often project a concrete image of evil, perhaps an angry old man with horns growing out of his head who lives in fire. But simply put, the ego is nothing more than the "wrong-minded" side of, or corner of, or piece of, the *whole mind*; it's the piece that made the error of dreaming up a separate thought from that of reality. Reality is complete and absolute wholeness, no matter how you choose to look at it.

This erroneous thought of separateness, called the separation— concretely seen as the "bite into the bad apple"—gave birth to the first tick of time and *abstractly* is merely only an instant of eternity. This is the instant we live in now, and because of this error, the ego is always fighting for dominance. It is filled with guilt about something always, and makes itself judgmental as a defense tactic. With all this talk of the ego and its ways, I'll bet you can think of someone at this very moment who fits the mold. If so, it is the ego in you doing the molding.

Have you ever decided not to speak to someone who has upset you because you don't like his or her stance on a controversial issue? Their position on the matter seems to threaten you and your position; therefore, you immediately start thinking of ways to defend your ground. Or have you ever felt ashamed for some of your own poor behavior, but instantly begin to conjure up excuses with a defensive thought, such as "This is my story and I'm sticking to it?"

This is all quite the opposite with the One Mind, or spirit, which only knows the abstract; it reacts the same way to everything it knows is true, and does not respond to anything else. Nor does spirit make any attempt to establish what is true. It doesn't have to. Spirit knows that what is true is everything that is real, unseparated, and eternal. The concrete ego has its reasoning for everything. The abstract needs no reasoning because it is exactly what it is. It cannot be altered, adjusted, or bargained with. It cannot be reinvented or diminished or exaggerated. It is Whole.

Chapter 5

The Shared Inspiration

Healing brings together what has been altered, and is a thought or a glimpse that you are more than just a body. It's a thought by which your mind can perceive a oneness beyond itself, and feel glad in realizing peace. It's elation. It's when abstract, right-minded thinking swiftly fills the gaps of the separated and cracked-apart concrete, bringing to it the abstract's touch. This elation reaches out to the One Child of God, which is the relationship of all minds called the Sonship. The Sonship is humanity as a whole, behind the dream of separation. You and I, and everyone you see, are what comprise the Sonship. The Mind behind this whole Son of God is the Christ-Mind. Some realize this already, but many are still unaware, given the ego's severe pull on them. God, which is the One Mind with One Thought as His creation, embodies the entire Sonship. This embodiment is all that is real; anything else is unreal and not of God. Therefore, what is not of God does not exist.

In order for us to see this more clearly through the ego's hold on us, let's use a concrete method many will recognize. Take a look at these two circles.

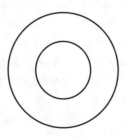

One circle is within the other circle. The One Thought of the One Mind of God is all that is within the larger circle, and within that is the Christ-Mind, which holds the Thought of the Sonship. Both circles share the sameness of being whole. Once you have accepted this visualization by your concrete thinking, where the ego runs rampant with questions, use your abstract thinking to remove the edge lines of both circles. Now you don't have circles at all, though the concrete part of you wants to still see perimeters. Inside the perimeters there will always be judgment. What can possibly be judged inside of infinity?

Anything seen as separate must have a perimeter. The ego wants to multiply, then divide perimeters for its accomplishments, making separate wholes and fragmenting off from that. This is its thought system. When the fragmenting begins by splitting the concrete thoughts, it leaves gaps where more perimeters are built. When abstract or right-minded thinking is alerted to this, it rushes to fill in the gaps, and perimeters cannot be built. This is the constant healing process that brings us wholeness, and is what you will be learning more about and experiencing as you proceed through this book.

When I was first arrested for my misbegotten business activity, I literally began losing everything I had worked for. This was all I could see. My conviction, which sent me to prison, stripped me of everything, including my dignity. I was lost, hopeless, and abandoned, as people, including some family members, turned their backs on me. The ones who stuck with me helped me to realize and look at the cracked-apart concrete that was in need of healing. In time, events started taking place, and people showed up when they were needed the most. Some bad experiences in prison hit me. The good that happened showed me how to forgive the bad, and I was also able to forgive those who had abandoned me. I was able to do so by learning to overlook the ego by looking beyond it. A very special friend out of my past stepped to the front—a surprise, without my asking—and has helped me to see that my faith and my fate had been right all along. He convinced me to see that I had just slipped up along the way, and that it was not too late to make whole of my errors. Because of this man's tremendous boost in my life, you hold this book in your hands. His name is Ron Skeen, and I cannot thank him loudly enough.

Since Ron's initial effort to reach out to me from his hospital bed following major surgery, a few others have jumped in to do what they can. This spurred on William Schenk to take positive action, and in a section ahead of us, you'll read how I met this brave man who endured more than any man of his age should ever be expected to. My point here is that this is how healing takes place. My right-mind continues to fill the gaps that the ego dug deep. I've learned to see no perimeters. Oneness is my vision.

The Holy Spirit uses time to help our right-mind think according to the laws that spirit obeys, and therefore honors only the Laws of the One Thought of all eternity, which is God. To your natural spirit, getting is meaningless and giving is all there is. With spirit already having everything, eternally, It loses nothing by giving, which enables us to create by extending, as our creator created us to do.

This kind of thinking is abstract and is totally alien to "getting" or "gaining" things—a senseless thought to the ego, where gaining is everything. Ego-based thought, or "wrong-minded" thinking, does not share ideas unless it is certain of its own gain; or it may sacrifice "now" for "future" gain.

If you share a material possession, you are dividing its ownership. If you share an idea, however, you do not decrease it. All of the idea is still yours, even though it has been given away. Further, if the one to whom you give it accepts it or sees it, it reinforces the idea in your mind and increases it. If you can accept the concept that the world is one of ideas, you are freed from the false association the ego makes between giving and losing—a limiting and detrimental belief.

So with this acceptance, or even a glimpse of acceptance of responsibility for your own false, or ego-based, beliefs, let's continue through the foundation for the lessons and messages of the remainder of this book. This will allow you to start filling in the gaps of the concrete and to recognize your own healing process, which will lead you to your true potential in achieving spiritual freedom.

Let's begin the path with a few simple concepts, which *A Course in Miracles* (ACIM) teaches us through its fifty principles.

- Thoughts increase by being given away.
- The more who believe in them, the stronger they become.
- Everything is an idea.
- How, then, can giving and losing be associated?

Your understanding of these concepts is your invitation to the Holy Spirit to be accepted as your Guide. Let me ask you to jot down these concepts on a small piece of paper or an index card, and use it as a book marker as you navigate through this book. By doing so, if you run into an area that may come across as too abstract for the concrete side of your thinking, these simple bullet points may help connect the dots, so to speak. The Holy Spirit is part of your mind, a part of who you are, and these concepts will help your awareness of this reality to become a more unified picture.

You will only experience the Holy Spirit when you invite Him to guide you. By inviting Him, you are acknowledging that He is a part of who you are. He is a part of the real you that does not die, but is still a part of your functioning body for communication purposes. He operates your right-mind and oversees healing the gaps of the concrete, which will gradually increase and extend your right-minded perception. One day, when all the gaps in all of humanity as a whole are healed, there will never exist another wrong-minded thought. The Holy Spirit is using time to strengthen this right-minded perception. When time has ended, humanity will no longer need the right-mind in eternity, because One-mindedness in its totality will be all that we live by. No need for dreaming any longer.

Jesus, the man who walked this earth, experienced these gaps and was able to accept total healing, and He brought the Holy Spirit into physical form through the dream. He manifested, or mirrored, the Holy Spirit of God to set the example, also by using time. Some individuals had, or now have, the awareness of Jesus's contribution. But many others along the way have abused His presence by interpreting it through the dream of form, only because of their own fears and lack of knowledge, due to the split-mind. The shift out of controversy and division has been a seemingly difficult task, but it doesn't have to be.

The Bible says, "May the mind be in you that was also in Christ Jesus." When this statement is reinterpreted by the Holy Spirit, it really means that we need to think as Jesus thought, joining Him in the Christ-Mind. Although egos may disagree, let's not associate the word "Christ" with a single individual. The abstract awareness, which Jesus was able to always maintain, was the Christ in Him—and it's the Christ in all of us. The "Idea," if you will, Christ, is the One Mind of God's Son, or humanity as a whole, behind the dream of separate identities. The entire Sonship as a whole operates by the Christ-Mind, with the Holy Spirit as our Guide, and Jesus, our elder brother, as our model.

God's Thought eternally extends His Idea, which Jesus names Christ and introduces to us. The Idea, or Christ-Mind, extends a thought, which is a sense of being guided. This thought, or the Holy Spirit, has been with us since the time of that first separated thought at the symbolic Garden of Eden, but the hold of the separation was so severe we could not grasp it or even glimpse it. This is why Jesus entered the dream of false ideas. Once again, please do not try to dissect this with concrete thinking, like an engineering project; but rather allow your abstractness to see the Holy Spirit in you as an Idea whose time has arrived. Truth will explode from you when you are able to take much emphasis away from your body and begin looking beyond to where your real thoughts originate. This place is the Christ in you, and the Holy Spirit simply points you in that direction. The Holy Spirit is doing the communicating.

He is referred to as the Healer, the Comforter, and the Guide, but trust your own abstract way of visualizing this, rather than what others may have pushed on you. In your own way, without performing surgery on this, look at Jesus, the man, as also one of God's Creations, whose right-minded thinking taught Him first that this Inspiration of Truth is within all of us, and is not separate or located somewhere outside of us. He would not have been able to have it Himself without knowing this. By allowing your own abstract alertness to flow, you are healing, and will begin to feel guided by the Universal Communicator as a realization, which will become a "knowing" based on your individual readiness.

The word "know" is proper in this context, only because the Holy Spirit can be viewed as the connecting bridge from our right-minded perceived notions over to knowledge. In other words, whatever you abstractly see in this tapestry I'm describing will be transcended to knowledge. But beware: the ego will immediately start trying to put concrete or bodily images in front of you as roadblocks. Once you have crossed over the bridge from any particular perception to arrive at knowledge, the gaps in your fragmented mind will continue to fill. Knowledge is always ready to flow everywhere, because it is everything that is real to you.

Look at it this way: Do you, or do you not, "know" when you are operating from truth? You don't perceive it; you merely know. But the ego does try to block this knowledge by "stretching" the truth, or "hiding" it. Once again, though, you do know of this when it occurs. You may hide the fact, but you do know, don't you? This is no different than when the clouds block the sun. You know the sun is really there behind the obstruction of cloud cover.

Try to absorb like a sponge, in the way that is right for you, that the Holy Spirit, in a psychological fashion, is the Thought that directs and guides your true essence. The *core* of what and who you are. He is aware of the knowledge you do and do not have. He is the protecting force, inspiring truth, oneness, and wholeness, leading you to complete and total healing.

Before the separation there was no need for healing, because no mind was separate and everything was abstract oneness. In the condition we now symbolically represent as Paradise, we were not comfortless, and communication was not necessary. Whatever tapestry you choose to paint of this for yourself is the truth.

The Voice *for* God, the Holy Spirit within us, is the Universal Inspiration—the call that brings wholeness to us—and when complete will be full Atonement, which is total correction and reversal of all errors. At this point in time there will not be a single fragmented or separated thought. Total healing of humanity's split-mind will have been achieved.

In the abstract, all of time is reduced to but an *instant*. However, if you wish to try to comprehend when full Atonement will happen, it will be the same millions of years away as was the separation. In other words, the dream of physical form will be over and we will have awakened unseparated, just as we have been all along. Nuclear or climatic or cosmic disaster cannot accelerate this event. The real, unseparated world, or universe, has no end. It sits right where it always has, within us.

The Holy Spirit will remain with us for as long as healing is needed, which is as long as time exists. When all minds have been healed—those behind us, with us now, and not yet in this world—this event in time will be known as the "Second Coming of Christ." It will not consist of a human body appearing on a mountaintop. This "Shared Inspiration" of the whole Sonship is now giving us, by the use of time, a tiny taste of Heaven—or eternal Oneness.

No one who experiences even instants of this state could ever believe that sharing it involves anything but gain. The condition of right-minded Oneness is incapable of attack, totally open, and in no need of defense, and knowledge is never blocked. It points us to the way beyond healing and leads our minds to live a life according to our own true free will, which, of course, is the Will of God. This is the Shared Inspiration.

Chapter 6

Setting a Clear Goal

Your Inspiring Guide operates simply and clearly. In fact, in order to be simple the method must be clear. The Holy Spirit sets a goal for us that is general. He will work with you at your invitation to make it specific. There are certain and specific guidelines He provides for any situation; but keep in mind that at first we may not yet realize their universal application. Therefore, you will need to use these guidelines separately as you become aware of them; and you will become aware of them gradually until you can safely look beyond each situation with an understanding far broader than you now possess. Healing the split-mind is an ongoing process for all of us.

I have found that my prison environment has accelerated my learning and healing process, due paradoxically to the constant uncertainty of daily life here. One never knows from one minute to the next when attack is going to sneak up from behind; surprising violence can erupt at any moment. In here I have literally survived by my constant use of "tunnel vision"—a one-track concentration on the principles of *A Course in Miracles*, which is why I believe I was able to absorb the material extremely deeply. You could say that I have lived completely within myself through this tunnel vision. I hope your life conditions are considerably more pleasant than my prison life has been; but let me share with you my own way for staying on the spiritual path. I am convinced that if it works in here, it will work for you anywhere you find yourself.

In any situation in which you are uncertain, the first thing to consider is this: *What do I want to come of this?* And next: *What is it for?*

In your ego's way of operating, no questions are asked. It will usually dive in and "go with the flow," so to speak. The situation becomes the determiner of the outcome, which can be anything. The reason is evident: The ego doesn't know what it wants to come of most any given situation. It surely is aware of what it does not want, but only that. It has no positive goal at all. We've all heard it said: "It looks like you walked right into that mistake." No one wants to fail or lose, but often failure or loss seems to be waiting for us.

Without a clear-cut, positive goal set at the onset, the situation seems to just happen, leaving all kinds of room for additional ego-based input. Though it makes no sense, the situation continues to develop. Then we look back on it with more ego-based, concrete thought, trying to understand or analyze our foolish thinking, or blame another person or group for the outcome. The ego may even tell itself how ridiculous it is. Not only is our poor judgment now in the past, but we have no idea what was truly intended to happen, because no goal was set with which to bring the means in line. At this point the only judge we have is whether or not the ego likes the way the situation turned out. It can sound like this: "Is this acceptable, or am I going to end up making a fool of myself?"

As a financial advisor I'd often worry about my performance giving seminars and lectures—stage fright, I guess. But I learned that people wanted reassurance that changes in their current situation were possible. If we feel our life is in the hands of fate, we will remain resigned, insecure, and fearful. But I found that when I focused on my own goal—to help people view themselves and their circumstances as improvable, regardless of what the markets appeared to dictate—not only was I more at ease myself, but the audience felt more at ease with my suggestions for ways they might work toward the changes that would give them a sense of steadiness in their lives.

The absence of a clear goal set in advance for the outcome you seek makes your efforts doubtful, opening the door for fear, and the goal never being accomplished. But not to worry; your Trusted Advisor will sort this out for you. You might be asking, "Where in hell has He been all along?" The answer is simple: He has been watching the ego beat itself up.

Speaking of berating oneself—and before I move on, so this might be seen a little more clearly—please bear with me while I share an experience I had in writing my first book, *The Master of Everything*. It may not seem to be a big deal at this particular time, however I offer it as an example of one of those battles we all contend with every day of our lives. I only laugh over this now because of the tremendous amount of healing I've experienced since. This also proved to me that the Holy Spirit was sorting out truths and falsities for me, and it did take some time.

Before my incarceration, while an investigation was being conducted on my criminal case, which led to my indictment by the grand jury, my attorney advised me to put a halt to my business travels and to sit tight, remain near home, and wait for the inevitable. He wanted me close by. At this point my career was over and my business was broke—twenty-five years as a financial advisor down the drain. While I stayed close to home, my tasks also included avoiding phone calls from bill collectors and coping with the mortgage company gearing up to foreclose on the house. I spent a good amount of time renting movies.

I had never been a fan of country music legend Johnny Cash, but decided to rent the movie about his life story, *Walk the Line*. I was captured by the way the movie portrayed him—that somehow the world had missed out on what a gentle and caring man he was. I was also impressed with the relationship he pursued and eventually developed with June Carter, who later became his wife. The movie motivated me to run out and buy a few Johnny Cash music CDs.

Fast forward to my incarceration in Belmont Prison, where I began my notes and writing to compile *The Master of Everything*. The ego in me was constantly reminding me that I was not in a position to undertake such a project. My heart was haunted by wrong-minded thinking, such as "Who am I to write a book, let alone a spiritual one?" I lacked computer resources and had only minimal access to a poor-quality typewriter, so my only choice was to start writing in longhand. But regardless, the urge set me to writing on a legal pad, then filtering and polishing my words before rewriting the text into composition journals I was able to purchase through the prison commissary. Those journals were as sophisticated as I could get until I could seek outside help, or possibly a publisher. I was thinking big, and my ego would tell me "too big." Naturally, all of this was very discouraging.

In recent years prior to prison, I had broken my right hand, the one I write with, and was told by the doctor I could expect some arthritis to set in and become a potential problem. Sure enough, he was right. After several months of writing what I called my "rough draft" or "comprehensive notes," I began to notice how sloppy and childish-looking my longhand writing appeared, and I was soon calling it "slop." I was becoming more and more disgusted with my "slop" and would often scold myself that "No one is ever going to want to read this slop." The pain the arthritis sent through my fingers, hand, and wrist didn't help my attitude.

Need I add that prison is a nasty, negative, dirty, foul, depressing, and oppressive jungle to live in? This place will destroy in a moment any flicker of optimism that the best of the most positive individuals could ever summon. My mental picture of my "slop" began to spread to my belief about the message I was trying to convey. "A bunch of slop that no one will ever want to read about." At what I then believed to be my midway point in this journaling effort, I angrily ripped the entire project to shreds and found the nearest trashcan. This little tirade could be compared to missing a three-foot putt to win a golf match against your buddy, and then proceeding to not only throw your putter, but your entire golf bag of clubs into the nearby pond. I told myself I was finished and sulked like a little boy for a couple of days.

Not surprisingly, if you know me, after that few days of sulking I was back up on my "writing horse," and something was burning inside me to simply start over and not worry about my poor penmanship. After all, I would be doing a lot of time in prison and I needed to use it to my advantage. I was told by my thoughts to just settle down, write at a slower pace, and get the message out, that somehow it would all come together.

One day, when an inmate who bunked near me was packing to go home the next day, he tossed a book onto my bunk. He was leaving it behind, and for whatever reason had decided to give it to me. It was about the life of Johnny Cash. While leaving a few things behind when being released from prison is normal and customary, this man had no idea whether or not I was a fan of Johnny Cash, and I really didn't think much about it myself. In fact, the book sat for a few days before I decided to page through it. But when I did, I particularly noticed a picture of a piece of lined paper, like from a legal pad, with Johnny's handwritten words to a song he was writing, which of course became a huge hit. The song was in the movie *Walk the Line*, and if you're ahead of me here, then you will suspect that I'm about to say that Johnny Cash's handwriting was indeed "slop." But I'm sure he never looked at it that way.

Chapter 7

The Goal Needs Faith

It's so easy to crucify ourselves over what seems to be important to us, when really it means nothing. My opinion of Johnny Cash's sloppy handwriting was merely my own opinion, no one else's. This is not something that was a negative in his life. The thought that struck me, quickly and deeply, was that no one who is interested in my message would care about my own self-declared sloppy penmanship. So why was I wearing the "crown of thorns" that I placed there myself?

The Holy Spirit sorted this out for me and suggested I remain focused on my message, which is important, and will one day be printed material, so my handwriting will have meant nothing. My point? This is how the ego sneaked in the back door to take advantage of my planless journey. However, the Holy Spirit used time and my experiences to create my vision of continuing from my own true *free will*, which is inner peace for myself, so I can share it. The writing of these books for now is simply one of the ways I am able to extend my free will to you, so that you may do the same.

The "slop" experience taught me the value of deciding in advance what I wanted to create, so I can perceive situations as a means to bring about my goals. Bad handwriting or not, the journey must continue because it is what I want—not what I *wish* for—and what I want explains itself as my true *free will*, with the explanation coming from God.

When we can make every effort to overlook whatever interferes with an accomplishment of our objective, and concentrate only on everything that helps us meet it, then what is happening will be quite noticeable. It is an approach by your Inner Guide to sort out the truth from the false. Yes, it was absolutely the truth that in the eyes of most people, my handwriting is indeed sloppy, messy, and can be childlike. But it is also *not* true that it has anything whatsoever to do with placing this book in your hands. The situation now has meaning, but only because the goal has made it meaningful.

The goal of truth has further practical advantages within your own self. If a situation is used for truth and for your own sanity, its outcome is always peace. In my case, my handwriting, in whatever form it may be, was a short-lived problem that I now laugh off as one of the ego's tricks that I was able to expose. Why did the ego, which is a part of my mind that is the root of wrong-mindedness, wish to trick me? Because it is the part of me that was once afraid of writing a book that may make a fool of me. Do you see how insane this *concrete* picture is?

If inner peace becomes the condition of truth and sanity, and cannot exist without them both, then where peace is, truth and sanity must be. Truth arrives of itself because it is always there and is always looking on. If you are experiencing peace, it must be because you are operating from truth, and you see everything truly. Therefore, deception will not prevail against you.

You will recognize a true outcome because you are at peace. This is where you will see the ego's way of looking at things. The ego believes that the situation brings on the experience, such as my poor handwriting being a mirror for my message.

But your True Inner Guidance System knows what the situation is, as the goal determines it to be, and is experienced according to the goal. In other words, my real goal, and not my poor handwriting, produced this book. And my poor handwriting served as a tool that allowed me to learn this lesson and persevere with my true goal and purpose. What I took in wrong-mindedness to be a flaw, in right-mindedness I see was a gift.

Remember, just as I must remind myself often, the Holy Spirit and the ego are both in our minds. The difference is that the Holy Spirit does not recognize the ego, because the ego is not real. It's an illusion, a false idea of life, whereas the Holy Spirit is of God and so are you. The goal of truth does require faith. Faith is the nature of accepting your purpose, which the Holy Communicator brings to you, and this faith is all-inclusive—meaning that there must be faith in the first place.

Chapter 8

Setting Your Goal Separate from the Ego

We all have the power within us to make a difference in our own life and the lives of others. Every situation in your life has certain aspects that you will try to address with substitutes. We can call these substitutes excuses, causing problems that arise from any given situation. Without excuses, the situation would not have been a problem. The substitutes do nothing for the situation, but they are a witness to your lack of faith. As such, now that you are on a path to right-mindedness, these lapses can become instructive once we learn how to recognize them.

The lack of faith *is* the problem, and it is this lacking you demonstrate when you remove it from its source—the ego—and insert it into the situation. You might place it into an attitude, such as "If only this were different," or "Who am I, anyway, to write a book?" As a result, you're not seeing the problem.

If it were not for your lack of faith that your problem will most definitely be solved, then the problem would be gone. The situation would have been meaningful to you, because the excuses would never have existed. When we try to remove a problem by placing it elsewhere, for example by using the excuse of blaming, all we are doing is removing ourselves from it. Therefore, it becomes unsolvable.

I already admitted to you that the reason I tore up my journal notes for my first book was to save myself from fear of embarrassment. Was I afraid of rejection? That fear was an illusion that caused me to remove myself from it by scowling at my own handwriting, then throwing it in the trash to save myself. The illusory fear kept me from having faith and enjoying the process of writing a book. If I had been enjoying the process and any situation in the process, there would not have been a problem. What was the problem? The fear, which is unreal and is not of God, therefore is nonexistent. God does not want us to be fearful.

Faith is real because it is of God, and it will solve all problems in any situation. You can shift excuses around all you want, but the solution will be impossible. Even if you shift part of the problem elsewhere, you will have lost all meaning to the problem. Would you dare to believe that all your problems have been solved in advance? If you answered yes to this, wouldn't this mean that faith must be what you are a part of when you knew the problem was already solved, and in advance? But if you answered "no" to this question, don't be discouraged. There's much hope for you only because you were honest in answering the question the way you see it. That, in itself, is faith; you're only misinformed by the ego. We all have faith, but it must be directed truthfully.

Look at it this way: A particular situation is simply a relationship comprised of the joining of different thoughts to meet a certain goal. The only real reason for problems to be perceived is because these different thoughts are judged by you to be in conflict with each other. By going with your heart in a situation, there can be no judgments resulting in conflict.

When I trashed my journal notes for the book project, I was not acting from my heart. Going with your heart simply means that all of the real you is feeling the truth, and you are sticking to it like glue. The truth inside you cannot be judged; however, it can be denied or delayed. If there is conflict in the joining of thoughts, some ideas of physical loss must have conspired. Minds cannot attack, but bodies and body thoughts can.

The thought of bringing bodies into a situation is a sure sign of faithlessness. Isn't this what happens when nations go to war with one another? Bodies cannot solve anything. But they can intrude on the relationship of these thoughts about the situation, causing error in the thoughts. This, then, becomes justification for a lack of faith in the right-minded direction.

My body, my thinking brain that had my true essence trapped, intruded when I acted in destroying those composition journals. We make these errors often when we place too much emphasis on the body. But let's not be too concerned with that, or we'll only be increasing the emphasis. Rather, let's see the fact that an error was made, and errors simply mean nothing. Try to get used to that idea. The Holy Spirit will undo these errors with the help of your trust in Him, which is faith. To "undo" by the Holy Spirit means to correct without punishment. Additionally, the fact that you can accept an error for being only what it is, an error, means that you do indeed have faith.

Once you can convert faithlessness to faith, it will never interfere with truth. But faithlessness used against truth will always destroy faith. If you know you are lacking faith, this is good. It is telling you that you are aware of your error. Simply send this message back to the Holy Spirit, asking Him to restore your faith where it was lost, and don't look for it to be replenished elsewhere, as if you were unjustly deprived of it. As well, merely asking this of Him proves your faith. You see, there is hope!

Now that you have hope, think about this and learn from your own abstract thoughts. Let's say you think you hold a grudge against another individual, your brother within the Sonship, for what he has done to you. But what you are really blaming him for is what "you" did to him. It's not his past, but yours, that you hold against him. You lack faith in him because of what you were—faithless, just like him. Yet you are as innocent of what you were as he is. What never was is causeless, and is not there to interfere with truth. If truth was never there to begin with, then there is no cause in anything that is faithless. Cause is of God, and is truth. Therefore, there must be Cause for truth, and faithlessness is not truth. In fact, it is nothing and is unreal. Why? How can anything unreal be of God? How can faithlessness have a cause?

The Cause, which is of God, has entered any situation that shares its Purpose. The truth touches everyone to whom the situation's purpose calls. It calls to everyone. There is no situation that does not involve your whole relationship with the One Thought of God—which is creation in every aspect, and complete in every part. In other words, being whole you are creation. When you think you are outside of creation, of the Mind of God, that's when you say, for example, "I must have been out of my mind." You can learn nothing of your real self outside of it. This truth shares the purpose of your whole relationship and derives its meaning from it.

Enter each situation with the faith you give your brother, or you are faithless to your own relationship. Your faith will call in others who were meant to share your purpose, just as the same purpose brought on the faith in you. This is why, after destroying my journal notes, I quickly restarted the project, and why the right editor and then publisher showed up at the right time. In this, you will then begin to see all the illusions you once had, transformed to means of truth, which is of your goal. Truth calls out for faith, and faith makes room for truth.

When the Holy Spirit changed the purpose of your relationship by exchanging yours for His, the goal He placed there was extended to every situation in which you enter, or ever will enter. And every situation has made you free of the past, because your real goals now make the past purposeless. Your zest for life won't need the past.

The communicating Thought of the Holy Spirit is both of and within you, wherever you go. It is you. Don't use faithlessness against it. This is the Thought that sets the goal of your free will apart from the insane beliefs of the ego.

Chapter 9

Making Decisions

We have covered a lot of ground so far in a quick time frame, and the goal now is for you to begin recognizing spiritual freedom through consistent methods for attaining it. However, you must acknowledge your faith in doing so. As spiritual teacher and author Marianne Williamson states in her book *A Return to Love*, "Hope is born of participation in the solution."

Your willingness to consistently participate will determine your fate in how far along the path you travel to spiritual freedom. The next chapters will offer you a few steps that will lead you away from the desire to judge, away from pain and suffering. They will lead you to forgive these desires. The steps may be new to you, but you must sincerely invite them to be part of you. Please be sure to look at them as merely ideas, however, rather than rules. Let's now discuss these ideas and try to ingrain them into your day-to-day routine. Welcome them into your home, so to speak.

The decisions we make are continuous, though we don't always realize we're making them. The amount of toothpaste you squeezed onto your toothbrush may be one of a thousand decisions you already made early in the morning, for example. We're not going to concern ourselves with saving toothpaste here; but for starters, we do want to practice seeing decisions so a new routine can begin to form. This will help you see the steps you never recognized as being important.

Please continue to read through these instructions no differently than how you've been reading this book so far. Don't let yourself become preoccupied with every step you take, because any incessant thinking will open the door for the ego to slam its input onto you. If you try too hard to study or dissect this practice, you'll surely raise questions for the ego to help you answer. In other words, take the little steps but don't ask yourself why or try to analyze their purpose. Simply participate in the step. Now, with this understood, let's move on and allow this section to simply flow through your Inner Guidance System, where it will be absorbed like a sponge.

Before going to sleep for the night, simply tell yourself that when you awaken in the morning, you will not be making any decisions about your day ahead of you. Then, when you wake up, you should have a mindset, and this will give you a good start. If you have any resistance or you lack dedication, you are not ready. If you're not ready, that's okay; simply tell yourself the truth that you're not ready. The honesty with yourself will give you the inspiration needed to start over tomorrow. Merely accept that you are going to try again tomorrow.

If you are truly ready, then think about the day you want to have. Not what you *wish* to have, or would *like* to have, but what you actually *want* to have. Tell yourself in an easygoing and gentle manner that *"There is a way in which the day I want to have can happen automatically."*

Take a few meditative breaths, making yourself relaxed. Then say to yourself a few times, until all judgment thoughts have left you, *"Today I will make no decisions by myself."*

This means you are choosing not to be the judge of what to do. Also, you are not to judge the situations where you will be called upon to make a response. If you judge the situations, your split-mind will apply the rules it has determined for how you should react to them. Then you will have another set of answers, producing confusion, uncertainty, and fear.

Our concrete thinking wishes to make all decisions for us; once we begin to judge, what we get is a response from the ego, resolving nothing. The judgment of the ego contradicts what you initially perceived, making you feel attacked. This creates a vicious circle that leads you to fear and anger. This has been the problem for most individuals. So for now, simply see your split-mind as your indecisiveness over all your thoughts. We'll go into this in more detail later.

There are some consistencies you must prove so this "vicious circle" doesn't arise for you. What I just described does indeed happen at first, while you are learning to hear the Voice of the Holy Spirit. For myself, I hear His Voice as a thought that is crystal clear and absolute, that brings joy and an enthusiasm that is full of brightness. All I can say for you is that you will know His Voice. So please accept all of this as learning—just as when you were learning to walk and had to fall at first for a period of time, but stayed with it because you had faith it was a worthy goal. Throughout the day, at any given moment you think of it, tell yourself again the kind of day you want to have. Tell yourself the feelings you want to have, and the things you want to see happen to you. Say: *"If I make no decisions today by myself, this is the day I will be given."*

The procedures are simple, and practiced well with truth will let you be directed without fear. The simplest part is the most important, which is being truthful with yourself. Any opposition that may arise will not be a problem. You must remember that any opposition is operating from the ego, sprouting through the cracks in the concrete, the gaps of separated thinking. But not to worry; this is no match against the truth that shines from within you.

By being alert but not alarmed, there will still be times when you will judge, just as a child falls when learning to stretch her walk farther. Your judgment will provoke attack within yourself, such as berating yourself with name-calling, unless you quickly straighten out your mind. When my daughter Erin walked at nine months old, we would lovingly laugh when she fell down. In turn, so would she, and her inspiration to walk without making her parents laugh became her goal. When you catch yourself beating yourself up with name-calling, stop for a moment and laugh at the fact that you have exposed the ego.

Start doing this by acknowledging any judgment you made. Remember, anything you try to *make* is of the ego, and what you *create* is of your true free will. Your acknowledgment of this will be enough; your judgments occur because you are unwilling to sit back and wait for an answer from your Advisor. What you have been used to doing is automatically deciding for yourself, based on concrete, wrong-minded thinking. Now you need a quick restorative before you ask again, so you can start to receive answers that flow through abstract thoughts. These are the thoughts that are of wholeness and the Oneness of Thought you were created from.

Remember once again the day you want to have, and recognize that something has happened that is not part of it. Then realize that you have a question by yourself, which was a decision, and you set an answer in your concrete terms. Then say to yourself, *"I have no question. I simply forgot that I don't decide by myself."*

This cancels out the concrete terms that you have set, and lets the answer show you what the question must really have been.

Try to observe this idea right away, despite your opposition. By now you may feel a bit angry. Your fear of being answered in a different way from what your version of the question asks, will gain momentum, but as you set it aside you will come to truthfully believe that the day you want is the one you are going to get. This is because now you will know that the day will be destroyed if it's not what you really want. Also keep in mind that the abstract cannot be forced or engineered, as with the concrete. It must become natural.

If your fears are still gaining momentum due to your decision making, you may have trouble realizing it. This is so because you have decided by yourself on the ideas that promise you a happy day. The decision can be undone by simple methods that you can accept.

If you are unwilling to receive because of the fear you have of an answer, then don't even ask a question about your day. You can begin to change your mind with this: *"At least I can decide I don't like what I feel now."* This much is obvious and paves the way for the next easy step.

By having decided that you don't like the way you feel, what could be easier than telling yourself this: *"And so I hope I've been wrong."*

This works against the sense of opposition within yourself and reminds you that help is not being thrust upon you, but it is something you need because you don't like the way you feel. This small admission allowing for help will let you go ahead a few more steps. This is no different from asking for a little push.

Now you have reached a turning point, because it has occurred to you that you will gain if what you have decided is not so. Now you know that what you decide on your own may be wrong, and so your happiness does not depend on your being right. This little bit of wisdom will now take you further. You are not being coerced, but merely hope to get a thing you want. Now you can say in perfect honesty: *"I want another way to look at this."*

Now you have changed your mind about the day and have remembered what you really want. Its purpose is no longer hidden by the ego-based belief that you want it for the ego-based goal of being right, when you are in error. Now you know how to be ready, but not in conflict, when you ask for what you want.

The final step is to acknowledge a lack of opposition. You are informing your open mind that you are willing to be shown by saying, *"Perhaps there is another way to look at this. What can I lose by asking?"*

Now you can ask a question that makes sense, and so the answer will make sense as well. Nor will you fight against it.

It is easier to have a happy day if you prevent unhappiness from entering at all. But this takes practice in the ideas that will protect you from fear. When this has been achieved, judgment, forever, has been undone. But meanwhile, you still have to practice the ideas for its consistent undoing. Now, let's consider once again the very first of the decisions that are offered here.

We've talked about beginning a happy day with the determination not to make decisions by yourself. This seems to be a real decision in itself, and it is. But still, you can't make decisions by yourself. Therefore, what do you choose to make them with?

Whatever you decide—however you decide things—you will not be making these decisions by yourself. Your decisions are either made with idols or with God. If you make your decision with what you have always idolized, the ego, it will help you to make concrete decisions that turn into confusion. Your day is not random and has already been decided for you. You must face up to this.

Your Friend who resides within you, and has been given to you by God, is by your side for advice, and He knows of your happiness. It is up to you to use His expert guidance, or not. If you do not, your idol, the ego, who is always in fear of something, will continue as it always has. There is no freedom in a decision you and your idol make. Why? Because it's a decision that is always uncertain. But your Expert Freedom Advisor and Guide sets you free.

Also, it is a fact that you and your Advisor must agree on what you want before it can actually happen. It is this agreement that makes all things happen. Nothing can be caused without some form of union, whether with a desire for judgment or the Voice *for* God. Decisions that are caused by you and your Advisor will effect the results you want for yourself, and for the world as well.

When you offer the type of day you want to the world, it will reinforce the idea of your Advisor in the world. Think about this, as well as the following question, before you move on in this book, and please keep it in the back of your mind: Whose world is this for the day you asked for?

PART II

HE USES LANGUAGE YOUR MIND CAN UNDERSTAND

Chapter 10

Inspiring Joy in Others

The stench of the county jail was inhumane, even as a most conservative description. In the corner sat the seventy-eight-year-old, white-haired man, sobbing all through the night. My initial take on the unshaven, grizzled guy was that he was an alcoholic vagrant doing a few days to dry out. Maybe a drunk and disorderly violation, I figured. Whatever his misdemeanor, he seemed harmless.

The noise echoed off the cement walls and solid steel door of the cell, a dank cavity infested with the germs and body odor of the sorry group of inmates packed inside, ranging from a DUI violation to violent criminals. One man was waiting for the transport bus to prison, where he would spend three years for car theft. Another, also waiting, had just been sentenced to life imprisonment for rape. This type of temporary and unnecessary dumping and holding is the norm for prisoners in transit or waiting for backed-up court hearings.

At that time I was there in transit *from* prison, waiting for a court hearing on technicalities of my own prison sentence. I expected my business to be finished by the end of the day I arrived, then to be sent back to prison. I had already been there waiting for three weeks. During this time I sat in this densely crowded jail cell with as many as twenty-five men at a time, when it was clear to see that the cell had been designed to sleep six. It contained only one toilet, one washbasin, one open shower, no windows, and a few rows of tiered metal slab bunk beds with floor cots between them.

Some of the men were on their way to other counties and some to other states. When the metal bunk beds were fully occupied—almost always—the floor cots were dragged in by new inmates and crammed into the thirty inches of space between each bunk. With barely enough space to move around, the tripping over and stepping onto others was a breeding ground for fights. I met men who, after a few days in such holes, fell into severe shock.

This is when I noticed seventy-eight-year-old William, who later asked me to call him Willie. Something inside me urged me to speak a few kind words to this despairing and broken Irish-looking grandfather type, with facial growth covered in dried blood. He explained that guards had dragged him from the initial holding cell to this cell. Handcuffed and shackled during the move, Willie, at his age, could not keep up with the guards' brisk pace, and he had fallen down a flight of three or four steps, landing on his face to the concrete floor. He had received no medical treatment or attention.

After a couple of days of watching Willie stare at the walls while leaning upright on his floor cot, I decided to approach him. He seemed relieved or comforted that during this horrendous time I was offering a few minutes to chat. We hit it off fairly quickly, as we each sensed a mutual helping hand in the other.

Through our conversations, and to my amazement, I discovered Willie to be very much a family man. His wife of fifty-two years had sadly passed away a few years prior, after a lengthy stay in a nursing home, due to a stroke. He had two loving sons who were close in age, and close to my age of fifty-one. Willie liked that about me. His sons had families of their own and were coping with the day-to-day struggles of balancing careers with family life. Their busy lives had blessed Willie with grandchildren and even great-grandchildren. The oldest of his sons had just left to go back to Oregon, but had been at his father's side when Willie was sentenced to go to prison.

Out of loneliness, Willie had remarried a woman about his age who loved to travel around the country with Willie in his motor home. They'd seen many great places together in the two years they'd now been married. His new wife's daughter was against the marriage from the start, however, and was causing a lot of chaos and grief in both their lives. She was concerned that Willie would squander her mother's nest egg and leave the estate penniless for herself as the rightful heir. Willie told me that he hadn't remarried for the money. In fact, he was doing fine financially, with his own pension from the post office and the estate he and his first wife had worked hard to build.

The new stepdaughter, about age forty-five, accused Willie of puncturing the tires on her brand-new Lexus with an ice pick that was found at the scene. Willie had been spotted at the crime scene by neighbors, which he openly admitted; he had gone to check out the area after he saw a gang of teenagers hanging around the new car. One thing led to another, and the stepdaughter was able to convince police that Willie was the culprit. Willie was charged with possession of a criminal tool (the ice pick), along with burglary. The very morning I met him, with his face covered with dried blood, he had just been sentenced to thirty months in prison.

When the incident first occurred, resulting in Willie's felony charges, he did not want to trouble his two sons or interrupt their family lives. They were both living out West, and he did not want his own adversities to become their problem. But Willie was in no way aware of the severity of the charges. He figured the whole mess could be straightened out by the public defender's office and saw no reason to get an expensive lawyer involved. He didn't believe the state would want to send an old man to prison. But he was wrong!

The state does want to send people to prison. In fact, the state is in the business of sending people to prison. This "prison business" involves big money; it keeps the law practices busy and the judicial system flowing.

The public defender who was assigned to Willie scared him into believing that if a jury found him guilty at trial, he would receive at least ten years in prison, partly to justify the expense of taxpayers' money to fund a trial. In this way the system convinces people who are innocent of crimes to plead guilty and accept a plea bargain. At his age, Willie was not going to chance this. Willie had never been in trouble before, and he trusted the public defender's advice to take the deal. Without telling his sons, he accepted a thirty-month prison term, with a possibility of being released early after six months.

I spent a few more days with Willie in the broiling summer heat of that oven of a cell, before he was transported off to prison. I gained an unusual, but bonding friendship with this all-American grandfather, and learned much about myself in the process of sharing our views on life. My thoughts were to one day look him up when this tough time in both our lives was behind us.

A few days went by, and it was my turn to be shackled and handcuffed and transported back to Belmont Prison, some two hours away. About ninety days later, on a day when a busload of new prisoners was arriving from the state's main intake and reception prison—a place to process new inmates into any one of the thirty-two men's prisons in Ohio—there was Willie, checking into housing unit #3, called "3 House." There are eight separate housing units at Belmont, each of which holds 272 prisoners, and they are always at full occupancy. Belmont alone had two busloads a week coming into the prison, which gives you a good idea of the large number of new prisoners arriving and ones being released: a continual revolving door.

What were the chances of Willie being assigned to Belmont, let alone to 3 House, where I was situated? It was once again a comforting meeting, and it was surely my pleasure to help Willie get squared away and to show him the ropes of his new prison environment, which can be very frightening. Prison is rough on everyone for countless reasons, and having a friend close by can make a world of difference. Was it a "coincidence" that Willie showed up at Belmont? I'll let you decide for yourself.

Willie has since served his thirty-month sentence in its entirety; he was denied an early release as promised by the public defender. I realize the public defender would have said that the court would "consider" early release. However, a prisoner in such harsh conditions will naturally take such a statement as an assurance; and Willie had certainly taken his attorney's advice to take the plea bargain based on the phrase "six months."

Willie writes to me often and has told me in detail what a feeling it was when his two sons both traveled from their homes out West to greet him as he walked out of the prison gate. He was eighty-one years old when he was released—over an ice pick and punctured tires. On one side, a teenage prank for which he paid the consequences; on the other, the perception of a "punctured" estate. He doesn't have to worry about his wife any longer, since their divorce was finalized just before he was sent to prison. But Willie has let go of all that occurred with her and her daughter. He says he understands that it takes two to tango, and he has planted in his mind a message that says, "Let the old battleaxe be." Willie now tells me that he has "truly seen it all."

Experiences like this have shown me firsthand the bitterness that resides in the prison system. I have learned that few prisoners are able to show, or refuse to display, their true feelings due to fear and resentment of the injustices they have suffered themselves and witnessed imposed on others. This makes for rage toward prison officials and beyond, spilling onto other inmates and prison life in general. Routine injustice is deeply rooted into the "justice" system, which is used by many judges, prosecutors, public defenders, prison operators, and others for personal gain in public life.

Clearly there are many prisoners who do belong behind bars, but this situation is not about their debt to society. All my years I have been a proud American and a firm believer that democracy is the best system in the world. I have always realized that of course, as with anything else, it has its pitfalls and "bad apples." But now I have witnessed close up the other side, where a mockery of justice is being played out over money and power.

Judges and prosecutors are locking individuals behind bars for political reasons and gaining votes as they prove their "tough on crime" agenda, regardless of the accused's individual circumstances or due process. That is, of course, unless there is plenty of money to hand over to "iron out" a situation.

Prisoners do exaggerate, though often they do so out of a longing for change; this is the only way many can express their disgust. At first, I discounted most of the stories I heard. But, as with Willie, I discovered that many of these tragic tales were all too true. I can honestly add my opinion here that the Founding Fathers of this country, who wrote the Constitution and suffered to defend it, would be ashamed of what has happened to politics in the U.S.—and all for the price of personal gain. Please answer this question within yourself: Who is there in this United States of America today, or in the entire world, that you can choose as a role model for your children? Is there anyone at all?

I do believe there have been other factors involved in these criminal cases, and many who should be punished go free. But as the stories accumulated, and I checked them out as best I could, it was easy to see why sentencing disparity is the chief cause of all the bitterness in prison. If this kind of thing were occurring in other countries under communism or dictatorships, the bitterness would not be borne. In the "Land of the Free" and the "Home of the Brave," however, when these things continually happen, we are right to be angry at the travesty.

Take a look at the case of inmate George, the owner of a large retail shopping franchise. George shot and killed his card-playing partner during a game of high-stakes poker. Expensive lawyers were able to "iron out" a plea bargain from murder to manslaughter, and George received a four-year prison term.

Then there was Terrence, an illiterate young man with virtually no education, who was serving twelve years in prison for possession of three pounds of marijuana. Terrence was caught up in a bind: about to lose his home to foreclosure, with a wife and two small children. He tried his hand at earning cash as a "delivery boy" for a big-time drug dealer. He would not "snitch" on the drug dealer in order to get a better plea deal because he feared for the safety of his family. Since he wouldn't "cooperate," the prosecutor demanded he receive a maximum sentence.

Such injustices of the system are everywhere, though not in every case. In many cases justice has been served. But those numberless cases where this is not so are very painful, and the bitterness extends when one comes to know the victim face to face. It fosters rebellious attitudes toward the law, even among those who know they deserve their own sentences.

Often it's the inexperienced lawbreaker, like Willie, who puts his trust in the judicial process and does expect to pay his debt to society for his or her error, only to be taken advantage of by zealous judges and prosecutors, who consign them to the prison system to meet demands that voters are totally unaware of. When are we going to bring into this land a system with the sole purpose of helping and protecting society, one that is not used to help deepen and fill up the pockets of the greedy?

This brings me to Doc's story. Doc told me he pled guilty without a plea bargain, just as I did. Doc was later told that his lawyer traded him off for another client with more money who could pay for "investigative expenses."

Doc had a small business that went belly-up, which put him behind on all his bills until he ran out of money. He could not pay for any "investigative expenses," and the lawyer suggested he hope for mercy from the judge for his child support arrearages, which had reached the felony level. When Doc contacted a government agency called "Child Support Enforcement" for help, they would not listen to him until he could get the following year's income tax return to prove his hardship. The "Enforcement Agency" had no choice but to report his arrearages to the court.

As Doc stood in front of the judge with no plea bargain at the sentencing, he noticed a patriotic banner hanging next to the American flag that said "The Land of the Free and Justice for Everyone." He said a quick prayer to God and trusted that the judge would treat him fairly. Instead, Doc was given a four-year prison term and was scolded by the judge for his "poor fatherhood" and nonsupport of his ten-year-old son. Doc told me that the judge had no idea how he did truly support his son, and that like many families, he had merely been hit by hard times. So now Doc is literally doing "hard time"—where he certainly has no chance of being able to recover or financially support his son. He writes to his boy often, supporting his son's dream of one day being an Ohio State football player. Doc is sure his son will achieve that goal. But "Child Support Enforcement" and the judge did not look at it that way.

What if we all were able to be increasingly aware of the Oneness we all share, and the Holy Spirit's constant communication between us all, in order that we may live our free will? We can't see Him with our eyes, nor hear Him with our ears, but He is there. How, then, are we able to recognize His presence?

When I first met Willie that day in the overcrowded county jail cell, we felt a sense of joy that inspired both of us. A connection, if you will. Most of us have experienced this before, but shrug it off as simply "having something in common" with one another. Does this seem familiar? Don't you think there's more to it than that?

If you inspire joy and others react to you with joy, even though you are not experiencing joy yourself, there must be something in you that is capable of producing it. If what is inside you can produce joy, and if you see that it does produce joy in others, you must be giving of yourself, and therefore are not lacking. In order to continue to not be lacking, you must receive the joy as well, which others have available in their "lackless" supply of joy. This is how giving and receiving can be seen as two distinct aspects of the same thought.

When we can begin to see this light on a larger scale, and incorporate this way of extending our thoughts in our pursuit to get a grip on crime, we can learn that what we fight we only get more of. Likewise, what we extend we get more of, and love is intended to extend.

Here is what legendary author Henry David Thoreau had to say in his famous book, *Walden*, about his experience of being jailed for not paying income tax, in a particular year when he was hit with hard times:

> You who govern public affairs, what need have you to employ punishments? Love virtue, and the people will be virtuous. The virtues of a superior man are like the wind; the virtues of a common man are like the grass; the grass, when the wind passes over it, bends.

Chapter 11

Your Bridge from Perception to Knowledge

A Course in Miracles states that "the way to recognize your brother is by the Holy Spirit in him." However, the ego tells us to "judge a book by its cover." How many times have we judged an individual, only to find the person to be totally opposite from our original perception of him or her? Just as with my perception of Willie sitting in the corner of that jail cell, it truly was the Holy Spirit's intention that I perceive him as a man drunk and down on his luck. Of course, I had a wrong-minded perception. But it was that wrong-mindedness that lured me to offer a few words to him. This is how the Holy Spirit will use ego-based thought.

The way we perceive a person or situation can be quite different once we gain true knowledge. Our journey starts with a perception. As we cross the bridge from perception to knowledge, we transcend our doubt, ending the journey at Home, which is knowledge. The Holy Spirit is the bridge we use to cross the gap. In my case with Willie, the urge I felt to say a few words began a conversation, and the Holy Spirit began bridging the connection.

We can use perception and knowledge, as they are related, because in the Mind of the Holy Spirit both are used where healing begins. Therefore, it is important for you to be aware of what is happening when you perceive. Think of how satisfied you feel when you no longer perceive a situation that had you hanging onto uncertainty, when now you know the truth, regardless of your initial take on a matter, issue, or individual.

All healing takes place through the Holy Spirit; therefore, He is the Idea of healing. This Idea, which occurs through thought, gains momentum when it is shared. Thought is a call of God. It becomes ego based only because your separated mind twists this thought into its own, insisting that it makes its own ideas. Remember, we are the Thought and the Idea of God.

The Idea of the Holy Spirit shares the substances of other ideas we have because it follows the laws of cause and effect, which these other ideas are as well. Why are all ideas a part of cause and effect? Because the law means that everything happens for a reason, and the reason has its purpose, or function. Within this universal law is cause, which is all that is of God. There, cause has its effects.

The substances of my meeting Willie could be, for example, the stench of the jail, my concerns for this old man's survival, along with my perception of him being a drunken vagrant. Additionally, he could have carried a substance, "the thoughts of his two sons," which I may have reflected. Substances like this can be an endless array of cause and effect and can also entail His use of time. In fact, without cause and effect, there would be no such thing as time.

There are two opposed ways of perceiving your brother, which are both in your mind, because you are the perceiver. These opposed ways are also in his mind, because he is perceiving you. See him through the Holy Spirit in his mind and you will recognize him in yours. How is this? By seeing him without judgment and only with acknowledgment as a son of God. What you acknowledge in him, you will be acknowledging in yourself. This means sharing, and what you share you strengthen. Try to remember that acknowledgment is needed; judgment is not.

The Voice of the Holy Spirit is weak in us; we must share it where we can recognize it in order to strengthen it. When we are not hearing His Voice, this is because of our unwillingness to hear it at that moment. We all have been trained by the world to limit our willingness for anything that is not of ego-based desires. Now, please pause for a moment or two and think about all of your desires.

Surely, many of us wish to have the finer things in life, the wonderful material possessions that satisfy and give us comfort. It's okay; we are rightfully due these things. But we are taught to believe that the ego's mindset of "Life's a bitch, then we die" or "Get all you can now because life is too short" is the proper attitude to adopt in order to meet the demands of other egos, so we can achieve what our little hearts desire. But this is a huge trap that will catch us always "wanting more." Whatever we have or do will never be enough, and the wanting of more will always produce fear.

Our all-loving Creator wants us to achieve and wants us to have a life of abundance, to be happy and comfortable. This is why he gave us His Holy Spirit as a permanent fixture within our mind. We are meant to gain in a fashion where nobody loses and everybody gains by operating from our own free will, which is God's Will. Truth will give you this happiness and will also give you what your "big heart" truly desires. You will have all that you want through giving, and it will be made possible by the Holy Spirit. What you want is your free will, and you will need certain things in order to get what you want.

What are those things? You will need an open heart that is not afraid to show honesty, faith, and respect for yourself and others. For example, before I decided to write this book, I needed to understand why I was writing it. Pain, curiosity, and my desire to extend the truth in me motivated me to share what I have learned through examining myself. But I've always been a private person, and I was now offering a display of my vulnerabilities. What has come over me to do such a thing?

I believe if readers can see parallels to themselves in me, I may help them feel less alone and damaged—just as my goals have transpired due to the help of others. After all, we're all in this together, right?

Truth is constant and it does not delay. It's always there and goes nowhere. It doesn't even take a break to "stretch" itself. When you are living a life of truth in every aspect of your "wanting," you will no longer be *wanting* because all of your needs will be met.

Delay is of the ego, because time is its lifeblood. Both time and delay are meaningless in eternity, which is where you always are, when you're living in truth. You are eternal. Your ego and its "substance" will turn to dust one day, and when this does happen, where will you be? Your body will be decaying and rotting away. But what about you?

You will be in the same eternal place you always have been. You only need the Holy Spirit while you are occupying this body. This is so because you need the Holy Spirit to give you communication from God, while the ego is running the dream of separation, which you are in.

Yes, that's right. Your dream of life is a section of the Christ-Mind that has slipped into a daydream of sorts. The dream thinks it can better itself by being separate from the One Thought of God. As we discussed earlier, this is what the Garden of Eden is really meant to symbolize. There is no reference anywhere that Adam ever woke up from the deep sleep the Bible portrays. In his dream, the "Tree of Knowledge" was violated due to a "wanting" with no involvement of truth, which is really "wishing."

The dream of separation can be compared to lucid dreaming, where part of our mind is consciously aware of the dream while we are having it. The part of the Christ-Mind actually doing the dreaming has a perfect alibi: this sleeping part is really not there in the dream; it is at Home with God, sleeping comfortably. As in all your dreams, you are the main character present, who you think to be your real self. But this character, or ego, is merely a representation of who you think you are.

This is why God has given us His Holy Spirit: so truth can be communicated to us, as the Holy Spirit whispers loving thoughts into our mind as we slowly awaken. Think about it. Do you try to awaken your dreaming child by frantically shaking her and abruptly turning on the lights? No, we speak softly and touch her gently. The Holy Spirit is awakening us slowly and comfortably, making us feel peace and joy and conveying understanding of what is true.

Remember, where we truly exist in eternity, while we dream, there is no time, such as in the concept of awakening "slowly." The Holy Spirit only uses time where it is understood by the part of your mind that dreams. All messages He reminds you of are in direct opposition to the ego's notions, because true and false perception are opposed to each other. There is no truth in the dream, and you dream of perception. However, there is truth in what He is teaching you as you slowly awaken. This part—your right-mind—perceives truly.

The Holy Spirit has the task of undoing our separated mind, and first He must undo all of our false perceptions. To do this, He uses the same methods of operation the ego uses, except with truth. The method is through a "feeling of realization" that is understood by our abstract thoughts. Much of our belief in falsehood stems from things that cannot be physically touched. These are our concrete ways of learning. The concrete is where false perceptions are born—just like my first take on William in the jail cell.

A step now for you in perceiving truth is your understanding that one level of your mind is not understandable to another level. Wrong-minded perception, or the ego, does not understand right-minded perception, or the Holy Spirit. The ego, believing in time, does not recognize the Holy Spirit's knowledge of eternity. The Holy Spirit has compassion for this condition, however, and as we already said, the Holy Spirit does have a function for His use of time, which is to arrange events within the dream. This is necessary in His slow awakening process.

Time is a belief of the ego, so the lower mind, which is the ego's domain, accepts it without question. However, there is one aspect of time that the Holy Spirit shows us as eternal, and that is "now." Now is always now and is never past or future. When you walk up a flight of steps, each step you incur is "now," and no previous or future step is involved. The "now" is as close as we can exist physically to eternity. It gives us a taste of it.

Could it be said that when you focus on the now, you are witnessing eternity, where time has no meaning at all? Can we take this even further to say that wherever there is "now," is where our abstract thinking can see God? Yes, of course! "Now," ask your abstract thoughts what He looks like.

The Holy Spirit is the mediator between the interpretations of the ego and your knowledge of your own spirit. His ability to deal with signs and symbols enables Him to work with us on the ego's level and in its own language. Therefore, He performs for us the function of reinterpreting what the ego makes and believes, by using our own abstract thinking.

The ego is not evil, just illusory in its wrong-mindedness, dreaming of fantasy. The concrete is all the ego can see, because it's all it thinks. The ego has taught us for centuries to believe only in the concrete—for example that the Second Coming of Christ will be a physical event where an actual man will appear on a mountaintop, wearing a shield and a sword, slashing the bad to his left and protecting the good to his right side.

The Holy Spirit uses truth and knowledge, and uses an abstract sense to reinterpret the ego's "non-sense," for us to see that the Second Coming of Christ does not involve a man or a woman, but rather is merely the full awakening of all minds. Total Oneness will be realized. It will be an event where the One Thought by all will know of no gain or loss, good or bad. Duality or separation will have no meaning at all. This will finally be full and complete Atonement: the interlocking chain of all minds where all that exists is Love and Truth as one. Always "now;" eternity.

Chapter 12

The Holy Spirit as the Reinterpreter

Understanding is light, and understanding and light lead to knowledge. This is not the light you see with the body's eyes. It is the light that is your state of mind. Your state of mind is either seeing darkness or seeing light. The darkness is not you, but you are the light. If you see the light you are seeing your real self and not what the ego has made for you to see. The light is always there because you are always you, and the Holy Spirit is in this light because He abides in you: He is you. Many have not known this. It is therefore the task of the Holy Spirit in you to show you the Source from which your light emanates. Consider this: A ray of sun is a beautiful sight and so are you, and the ray of sun is one with, and of, the sun, from which it extends, or emanates.

In order for you to know spiritual freedom, you must take the step to have knowledge of that which you cannot understand yourself, alone. This is a must, because you cannot know freedom if you remain detached from your rightful place within the Sonship, which is of God.

You are not like the ray of sun alone, which the sun itself shines forth. All individual sun rays are illusory. There is only one ray emanating from the sun; however, there are clouds that cause the separation of that single ray. You and I and our sisters/brothers are that one ray that emanates from its Source. We must not fear the cloud that wants to cover us, hoping to keep us separated from each other and our Source.

This is your life, your eternity, and yourself. It is this the Holy Spirit reminds us of. It is this the Holy Spirit sees. When you begin to see this it will frighten the ego in you, because this type of vision is very calm. Peace is the ego's greatest enemy, because its reality is all about fighting for survival. This is why it wants to believe its flesh and bones will one day be called to rise, after it has already turned to dust. This and many other beliefs are its only way of seeing itself to be eternal, and the ego strives hard to maintain its illusion. But even in its strife it is fearful, because its illusions cannot protect it from the unknown.

If you believe there is strife in you, then you will react viciously, because you have the idea of danger in your mind. The idea itself is an appeal to the ego. The Holy Spirit is as alert and watchful as the ego to the call of danger, opposing it with His strength, just as the ego welcomes it. The Holy Spirit counters this welcome by welcoming peace. Eternity and peace are as closely related as time is to war. Eternity and peace will always win because they truly are all that exists. When a war is over, regardless of who won or lost, eternity and peace are still your residence, unchanged and unharmed.

The ego uses perception to create meaning. The perceptions you accept become the foundations of the beliefs you will make. The separation, or split-mind, would not exist if it were not for perceptions. The ego is the symbol of separation, just as the Holy Spirit is the symbol of peace. What you perceive in others you are strengthening in yourself. You may allow your mind to misperceive, but the Holy Spirit lets your mind reinterpret its own misperceptions.

The Holy Spirit is the perfect teacher. He uses only what your mind already understands in teaching you that you do not understand it. He can deal with a reluctant learner without going counter to the learner's own mind, because part of that mind is still for God. Reluctantly or not, we all long to learn. This is why the Holy Spirit wants you to tell Him when you are frustrated and not at peace. He doesn't expect you to figure out the solution.

Despite the ego's attempt to conceal this part of your thinking, the reluctant learner in you is still much stronger than the ego, although the ego does not recognize this. The Holy Spirit recognizes it perfectly, because in the learner is where He abides;

this is the place in your mind where the Holy Spirit makes you feel at Home, even while you still dream of separation. I felt this myself when I was overwhelmed by failure and threat and discouragement, but still felt things would work themselves out.

You who are part of God are at Home in His Peace, except when the ego interferes with separate thoughts or wrong-minded perception. This is the illusion beginning, which the Holy Spirit is undoing. The ego made the world as it perceives it, but the Holy Spirit, the Reinterpreter of what the ego made, sees the world as a teaching device to bring us Home, which merely is to reawaken.

The Holy Spirit, only for you, must perceive time and reinterpret it into the timeless. He must work through opposites, because He must work with, and for, a mind that is in opposition. Thus he will correct and we will learn, as we are open to learning. Our separated mind did not, of course, make truth, but truth will set us free. Look as the Holy Spirit looks, and do not be afraid of your abstract thoughts, and then you can understand how He understands.

The Holy Spirit is of God, part of you. He is your Guide in order that you achieve your own free will. He is holding the remembrance of things past, and all there is to come, and brings them to the present for your benefit.

He will use thoughts of your past along with what He knows the future holds to arrange events in order that your free will be fulfilled. He is doing this for you because your achievement of free will is necessary in order that your brothers and sisters achieve free will as well. The achievement of free will, whereby everyone is fulfilled, is all about our part in the interlocking chain of Atonement. Its completion is guaranteed by God, regardless of the ego's strife.

Chapter 13

There Is Another Way of Looking at the World

At this point in our transition to spiritual freedom, we need to develop an understanding that our Source, or God, is within us and does not reside in a location "out there." The perception seems to be of "God up in Heaven" or "Let God hear you cry out to Him," as though He is somewhere outside to reach for. The world has done a great job of programming this belief or perception, which comes from the concrete thinking of the "hard-headed" ego. This promotes the "fear of God" as we "cry out" for salvation. This fearful perception leaves us with uncertainty and dread of the unknown. No wonder we are all filled with doubt.

You will need to see the bridge over to knowledge before you can take a single step toward the truth, which will set you free of any and all doubt. You can begin your journey by making a shift in your perception, from outside yourself to within yourself, by using the following exercise each day for at least twenty-one days. It will also be a great idea to continue beyond the twenty-one-day mark, as you feel the need for maintenance.

The idea is to start out slowly and gradually attain the goal of recognizing the majority of anything you perceive as within, and from within, your mind. Also the goal is to enable you at a moment's notice to move any outside perceptions you may have to within your internal, or natural, realm. With the help of the Holy Spirit, you will learn to bridge the gap from perception over to knowledge. This can only be done from inside and is impossible from outside yourself.

EXERCISE #1

Start out your day by taking five minutes to yourself each morning at a time of your choosing. Be sure it is a time you can feel comfortable and unhurried, with no anxiety.

Take a look at the outer world going on around you without judging it. It can be anything at all, from a car going by in the background to family members getting ready for their day, or even thoughts about your day ahead. Once again, do not judge any of it as good or bad; just survey it.

As you notice these happenings, quietly say to yourself: *"There is another way of looking at the world."*

Then quickly shift your attention to your inner world, that which is going on inside you, in your mind.

Repeat the statement: *"There is another way of looking at the world."*

Next, start alternating between surveying your outer and inner perceptions, but do so very calmly, without being abrupt. Merely glance casually around the world you perceive as outside yourself, then close your eyes and survey your inner thoughts with equal casualness. Try to be equally uninvolved in both as you conclude the five-minute session. Try to look at this five-minute period each morning as a personal time with yourself.

As you proceed through your day, use this exercise in a more informal manner in any "down time" you may have or whenever you find yourself feeling rushed or disturbed—for example, stuck in a traffic jam, or standing in line at the bank or post office with an obnoxious person in front of or behind you.

It's important to maintain a feeling of detachment from your outer and inner worlds as you say to yourself in the slightly shorter version: *"There is another way of looking at this."*

Remember to apply this idea the instant you are aware of distress. It may even be helpful to take a minute or so and sit quietly, repeating this phrase to yourself while closing your eyes and using a favorite breathing technique.

This phrase can also be turned into a meditation at any time. Simply repeat to yourself, aloud or silently, *"There is another way of looking at this"* as you survey your inner and outer worlds without judging a thing as good or bad.

Please make sure you do this exercise for the next twenty-one days, and continue after that as you feel it necessary.

What you will be doing is learning, more and more each day, to have your perception come from your inner world, rather than the outside. The more you live from within this realm, the more you will be living from truth, which is pure knowledge.

Chapter 14

Your Mission for Your Brother

The deeper you take the daily exercise "There is another way of looking at the world," the more in touch you will begin to be with your mind. You will start noticing the ego's frantic voices disguised for different situations. As you start recognizing this in yourself, you will also start to willingly undo the messages the ego gives you.

For example, the obnoxious man behind you in line at the post office may only initially seem obnoxious, and within a moment or two you will understand he is simply having a bad day, as you have had yourself. Or, if his hostility is so bad that he just doesn't give up, you may find yourself simply and quietly leaving the post office for another time in the day, without making a big deal about it. This is the Holy Spirit in you, the calmness that does not put a rush on the task at hand, while realizing that nobody really likes standing in line at the post office anyway.

As I talk about the Christ in you, I am not meaning "in" your body, but I do mean in "you." The Christ in you is not outside yourself. Anything physical about your body, including your internal organs, and even the cells and atoms, are outside of who you are. The smallest molecule in your body is a part of your flesh and bones. These microscopic body parts are your physical body, which is the framework for who you are. Just as the sun is the center of our physical solar system, by now I hope you are focused on the fact that you cannot be separate from what is at the center of you. What gives you life cannot be centered around death. Your body, cells and atoms included, is going to die. You are *not* going to die.

Your holiness is not your flesh and bones, but your holiness is who you are. This is Christ. The Christ in you is what will never die. Your body is merely a temporary structure, a communication device the Holy Spirit uses. Nothing more, nothing eternal, and nothing fearful. All of this wrapped up together is your holiness.

With that said, who and what you are is at one with Christ, whose purpose is to make manifest, or to be seen through you by those who don't know He exists. How you reveal Him is in the way you reveal your true self, thereby allowing others to see Him through you.

Now we can easily understand that when it is said that "Christ is everywhere you go," it literally means physically "everywhere you go." This is why for the time being you are occupying this framework of flesh and bones. However, once communication has been established by the use of your body, you indeed go places without your body. How many times, when an important decision was needed, did you remember something that an old friend or family member once said? Or have you ever been thinking of someone when the telephone rang unexpectedly, only to be that person, or a letter or email showed up that day? The response we have when this happens seems to always be, "Oh my God, I was just thinking about you!"

Do you as a son of God, and not meaning of flesh and bones, abide everywhere? Of course you do, and this is because the Christ-Mind that you are a part of is everywhere. If you are a bit confused here, as to how you can be everywhere, you may still have too much attachment to the body, or ego. Try to think of yourself this way: When you turn to dust, meaning of course, your body, where are you then? This will make more sense to you in time, which the Holy Spirit is using at this moment for this very purpose.

The mind that thinks it is a body is split, and this is where healing is needed. This occurs naturally, of course. Regardless of what the ego tells us, our abstract thoughts are naturally a part of the healing process. So go ahead, have them, and without guilt. The concrete only cracks apart with time. Our process, or journey, as the Christ-Mind accepts the Holy Spirit's remedies for healing, builds the bridge that crosses over the gaps or splits of perception to knowledge. Nothing that preaches, or ceremonies themselves, can make the Christ in you manifest. You must announce to yourself that healing is needed, and those who also know Christ will acknowledge this in you, thus helping the healing process. The others will gradually learn to see themselves through you and will gradually know Christ in their own selves.

God is not separate from us; He is the love inside us. He creates His miracles through the Christ that we all are, using the Holy Spirit as the communicator within this realm, where He uses cause and effect to bridge the gap, sending love on its way. All of this takes place within the Christ-Mind, at one with God, Who is the Maestro of this one magnificent symphony orchestra.

Chapter 15

What Is Within Must Be the Teacher

From the callus on my writing finger that prevents further blistering; to the letters of encouragement I receive, asking me to "hang tough" here in prison; to the memory of my daughter's first bicycle ride; to all the little but meaningful happenings in each of our lives: This is the face of Christ, which is not a physical body.

Here is a story of a woman I have known for many years, who is about my age. She was responsible for my getting into the business I maintained for twenty-five years. In recent years we had totally lost touch with each other; however, through the modern computer age, she was able to learn of the situation that sent me to prison. Connie has written me a few letters of encouragement and has, of course, given me the details of her story, which I'd like to share with you.

An event in Connie's life many years ago, although meaningless to the world at that time, has made a difference in the lives of many children today, around the world. Anyone who helps others discover the impact of the Holy Spirit, helps themselves, helps others, and helps the world move toward being a better place. This increases the vision for those who are ready.

In her efforts to keep me inspired, my friend Connie shared with me the facts about an individual who made a difference in her life, which has helped her to help others. I was so glad to hear from her.

Connie was twenty-three years old at the time of her story and trying to "chip" her way into the art world as a sculptor, while involved in painting as well. Connie is very talented, and she was determined to acquire her art degree from the world-class school she was attending. I remember the studio apartment with a fireplace where she lived. One damp winter night, when the wind was howling off Lake Erie, she longed for a fire and a good book. Instead, she had to turn in her final exam project at the art institute. Her professor, a world-renowned artist himself, was wrapping up his year at the institute and was on his way back home to Paris. The next day her project was due for her final grade, and it would be the last time she would see the professor before he returned to France.

I can remember her telling me of the excitement that filled her, when at the end of the class the professor dismissed everyone, but asked Connie to stick around for a few minutes.

"I'd like to put a grade on your project right now," he told her. She thought it an odd request, as normally the professor could take days to grade a project of this magnitude, but she obliged him. She had no idea he was about to change her life.

As he handed her the grade, the professor said to her, "Connie, I want to talk to you about your future. I've taught around the world for a long time. I've seen lots of students pass through my classes." He smiled kindly. "You are one of the brightest of those students, but you don't know that about yourself." Next he got serious and to the point. "As you leave here tonight, I want you to remember my words: You can do anything you want to accomplish. Before we part ways, I want you to promise me you will accept this within yourself."

He gave her the telephone number of a well-known art gallery owner in New York City he wanted her to contact. He told her to use his name as a reference.

His words burned into her memory when she realized he had no motive other than her best interests. She thought about this deeply, working hard on her schoolwork and juggling both a job and school. She managed to graduate at the top of her class. After graduation she took a position at the well-known gallery in

New York City, where she began to meet the right people from all over the world.

At the time I am writing this book, she is blessed with her own art gallery, where many of her own exhibits are placed. Connie has been fortunate in working with other great artists and influential business people from all over. One of them is a publisher of children's books and teaching aids. But something was missing in Connie's life; she was unable in her younger years to have children of her own, which always troubled her. But she does have an adopted son, who is dear to her, now grown and on his own, and doing well.

Using her artistic talent, business skill, and her love of communicating at a level that talented and artistic children can understand, along with her wide-ranging professional resources, she now touches the lives of children around the world. Her instructional books, CDs, DVDs, and software are used by children who have a desire to pursue their growth in the world of art.

Connie would like to let her former professor know he was one of the most influential people in her life. The problem is, she found out he passed on a few years ago. Nevertheless, she senses that he smiles in a certain way.

Countless millions of individuals are just like that professor, every day validating and inspiring others, and there is a very high probability that in most cases they will never be told that they made a difference.

We all have been appointed by the Christ in us to carry out our own free will. Having the easy job that gets you by in life by paying the bills is not necessarily living your free will, though it could be. The job you have does not necessarily signify your free will. You will know it in your heart if what you are doing with your life is your free will or not. Surely you will know if you are fooling yourself.

This is really not about the job you have, which is necessary to survive, but about what makes you passionate about each day when you wake up in the morning.

Doing this task that the Christ in you has designated for you cannot be hard. It is He who is doing it for you. This is where your joy is in what you do. As you are living this free will, which is God's Will, you will learn that your body merely seems to be the means for doing it, and your mind is also His. Therefore, it must be yours. This is a unity of mind, which is your holiness as we talked about earlier, and directs the body through the mind at one with Him.

How else can you reveal the Christ in you, other than to accept this holiness of which you are? Religions have done a good job of teaching us about the holiness and the holy places "out there." This is where perceptions tell you that you are what you *think* and *see*. By praising a body you erroneously believe that you must attach yourself to, or connect with, what is "out there," and see it as a missing piece to the puzzle that special ceremonies, rituals, or interceding others will help you find. But no one and nothing outside you can fulfill this role.

To know your own spiritual freedom you must understand that the message and the messenger are one. You must see your brother/sister as one with yourself. Remember, the Christ in you is also the Christ in your sister/brother.

Your own ego-based perceptions are choices you make of what you want yourself to be, the world you want to live in, and the state in which you think your mind will be content and satisfied. This is why the ego likes to judge a book by its cover. This judging of others dictates how you feel safe. It reveals yourself to you as you would choose to be, which makes the ego feel in control. However, ego perceptions always reflect confusion and indecisiveness, which keeps the ego holding the reins to separation.

You are the means for God's Will, which is your will—not separate, nor with life apart from His. His Life is revealed in who you truly are. The holiness that you are is the frame for each aspect of your Creator. You and your brother/sister are these aspects. One frame surrounding one portrait. There is a radiance that shines through each body the ego cannot recognize. This radiance is seen by others who will accept it or allow their egos to turn away in confusion.

The ego, because it is confused, wants to hide the light and puts up a veil to keep it separate from the face of Christ. Since you believe you are separate, Heaven presents Itself as separate too. It even is seen as having a gate, to add further to its separateness. With this separate understanding, the link that has been given to you may not reach you.

God, the Son, and the Holy Spirit are One Mind, and all of your sisters/brothers join as the Son and in truth. Christ and God have never been separate and never will be. Christ abides in your understanding in the part of you that shares God's Will. The Holy Spirit links the other part, the mad little desire to be separate, special, and different from Christ. This linkage is very important, because it makes oneness clear to what really is one, as you and your sisters/brothers lift the veil. In this world of separation this is not understood, but can be taught.

The Holy Spirit serves Christ's purpose in your mind, so that the aim of specialness can be corrected where there is error. Because the Holy Spirit's purpose is still one with both God and the Son, the Holy Spirit knows the Will of God, and what you really want. Events will then start being arranged. But this is understood by the mind aware that it is one, and so is experienced as truth and knowledge.

It is the Holy Spirit's function to teach us how this oneness is experienced, what we must do and where we should go so it can be experienced—for example, the circumstance that caused you to come upon this book and the message you are receiving.

Regardless of whether or not you were aware of the Holy Spirit's workings, you did experience its message.

All of this takes note of time and place, as if they were discrete, while we think that part of us is separate. It is apparent that a mind so split could never be the teacher of oneness, which unites all things within itself. Therefore, what is within this mind, and does unite all things together, must be its teacher.

All of this can simply be reduced to a simple understanding, as the *Course* teaches us:

> What is the same cannot be different,
>
> and what is one cannot be separate parts.

PART III

WHERE YOUR SPIRITUAL STRENGTH IS DISCOVERED

Chapter 16

Are You Losing Yourself to Sacrifice?

As you repeat the words in the prescribed daily exercise, "There is another way of looking at the world," consider this statement from *A Course in Miracles*: "The world you see is based on sacrifice of oneness."

Since biblical times we seem to have built a world based on sacrifice, and we take pride in this. Before I continue, I wish to make it perfectly clear that I am a true believer in what the Bible can teach us. It may quite often come across to you that I contradict the Bible based on the teachings of *A Course in Miracles*. My only contradiction, however, is in the way the ego has interpreted scripture based on its concrete thinking, interpretations created and perpetuated by this fragmented ego-based thought pattern for centuries. This is why we paint pictures of God being an old man with a white beard, wearing a white robe, raising a staff in his hand to make lightning strike. This type of image adds to our illusory thought process, reinforcing illusory interpretations that broaden as time goes on, making them into fairy tales, so to speak.

We can learn to see the real world more often, in a more naturally abstract way, which will allow truth to become more natural. All we have to do is "let go." What you may see in the abstract will, of course, be different than what I see, but not separate. Truth is what we naturally are, and what we naturally are cannot be made. It is what it is. Nothing changes who and what we are, not even sacrifice. In fact, sacrifice can actually cover the truth within us.

For example, the concrete often sees sacrifice as a necessary means to gain something or to forgive someone. The thinking always seems to be "If we pray long and hard for hours, we will surely deserve a spot in Heaven," or "I deserve to have a beautiful home; after all, I did work my fingers to the bone," or "I am going to go out of my way to forgive her." The ego continually repeats these stories, insisting that this "sacrifice" is what God wants from us.

But such ego-based beliefs merely lead to the trap of increased separation and continued fragmenting of our already split-mind. This causes us more and more disunity and total lack of joining. Just take a serious look at how different religions have different ways of "guaranteeing" you your salvation, if you will only sacrifice "this" in order to gain "that." Even in areas outside of religion, how many of us are not suitable for "this" group or "that" group because of concrete ideas?

This is the disunity I am talking about; but we continue to think in concrete terms, and we are taught that the abstract is something "far out," when really it is "far in," as inside. Once again, the concrete sees Heaven as a place in the clouds with streets of gold and Saint Peter standing guard to decipher the good from the bad. Someplace you "go." This is concrete thinking. Is this "far out" or "far-fetched?" "You can find out for yourself," the concrete tells us, "if you sacrifice."

I came across a magazine article by Arun Gandhi, the grandson of Mahatma Gandhi, which gave new meaning to me about what happens within us when our thoughts tell us we must sacrifice in order to gain.

If it had not been for racism and prejudice and the slave trading of history, we may not have had a Gandhi. He may have been just another successful businessman or politician who could have eventually made a lot of money. He was urged by many to pursue a business path, making the necessary sacrifices to become a business leader.

However, because of prejudice in South Africa, he was subjected to humiliation within a week of his arrival. He was thrown off a train because of the color of his skin, and it humiliated him so much that he sat on the platform of the station all night, wondering what he could do to gain justice. He knew that in order to gain justice in his current frame of mind, he would have to make some sacrifices. From his business perspective, he was aware of how he could get even.

His first thought was one of anger, as he contemplated some form of attack to gain revenge, and through his attack thoughts he was seeing justice served. These thoughts were violent, but he stopped himself and said, "That's not right either." He realized that all he would be doing was losing part of himself to such action. It might have made him feel good for the moment, but it really wasn't going to win him justice.

His next thought was to go back to India and live among his people in dignity. He ruled that out also. He thought that running away from his problems was not the thing to do, and would be a loss to his purpose for being in South Africa in the first place. He looked inside himself for a peaceful resolution. This is when he started to pursue nonviolent solutions, and he practiced it in his life as well as in his search for justice in South Africa. He ended up staying in that country for twenty-two years, and then he went back to lead the movement in India.

This is the kind of sacrifice that has nothing to do with personal gain. I have seen over and over in my own life situations where conflict leads to verbal or physical violence, resulting in loss. It always seems to be a matter of who loses the most, with the winner ending up with more, and proudly assessing their own losses. It seems the harder the loss, the better the gain feels.

When we are contemplating attack, the thought of some form of sacrifice is a key idea. It is where all compromise plays its hand in desperate attempts to strike a bargain, and where all conflicts seem to achieve a balance. The principle of attack is that you must sacrifice in one area to gain in another: "Somebody must lose something." This is the focus of concrete thinking on the body and its attempt to limit loss. Even with the experience of joy, the concrete brings sacrifice into play. For example, "What goes up must come down" is the concrete way of understanding that there must be "doom" around the corner. The abstract does not have "flip sides" to such ideas. There is no opposite to joy, peace, love, or oneness.

When you believe in your body as your domain, the body itself becomes the sacrifice, because of these concrete beliefs determining what is real and what is unreal. But ask yourself this question seriously: Where is your concrete way of looking at things going to take you, when your body makes its last heartbeat? Would it not start the process of turning to dust? How concrete is it then?

You see a brother as his body, separate from yours, making your key idea to only see the little part of him that you want to see, and sacrifice the rest. Just take a look at the world and you will see nothing attached to anything beyond itself. Every entity will either come close to you or move farther away, but when viewed as of the concrete it cannot join.

Since humankind was symbolically cast out of the Garden of Eden, humans have gradually built a wall around their own "hard-earned" entities—bodies, homes, yards, towns, countries—making separation its newfound paradise. It looks as if whatever is within its "concrete" boundary can never extend outward, and what is outside must never join, keeping behind its wall. Each individual's own boundary must sacrifice the other side to keep itself feeling complete, in the wrong-minded belief that if they joined each other, each one would lose its own identity.

The concrete split-mind has chosen to view as "other" all that your body fences off in order to become "yourself," an illusory identity created through your own sacrifice of the rest. You allow yourself to lose almost everything else to have an identity you can call your own. This you are sure the world will approve. When you have this perception of yourself, you proudly accept what you lose as a sacrifice, and the part you keep looks forward to more gain, making up for what it lost.

This, of course, requires more sacrifice. The thinking that the world proudly accepts is "No pain, no gain." With this, your belief in separation becomes doubly strong, glorying in its trophies— both the pain (sacrifice) and the supposed gain. But the little part of you that is left now places limits on everything "outside," just as those same limits are on everything you think is yours, even your own right to be truly joyful without guilt.

In one of my favorite movies, *City Slickers*, Billy Crystal plays Mitch Robbins, a disillusioned radio advertising salesman, who takes a much-needed vacation at a western dude ranch with a couple of longtime friends. At the beginning of the movie he considers whether he really wants to go, due to all the daily trials and tribulations of his life. He thinks the trip will be more trouble than it's worth. His wife disagrees, saying that he has sacrificed enough of himself to his career without a break and urging him to go find his joy for life, which he seems to have lost.

During the course of the movie, he comes to agree that he has lost something and starts to understand the value of laughter and having fun without consequences. At the end, when he gets home, he sees that nothing has really changed, but everything with him has. He has the same problems, but now having a zest for life, he is able to embrace them with a renewed sense of joy.

Many people today are in the same place Mitch was at the start of the movie. They have lost any joy they once had in their heart. The days ahead look flat and repetitive, as boring and monotonous as an assembly line. It seems to be the same old "concrete." Faced with this prospect of endless repetition, people lose themselves. They feel dull and believe that continued sacrifices are necessary so that one day they can have fun.

More and more people continue to say, "I just don't know how to have fun anymore." They're overwhelmed with life in general and see no prospects for change. But is this really true that they don't know how to have fun? For many people, "fun" has become an addiction. But as with most addictive substances, people build up a tolerance for it. So despite all the "fun" things people do, they are still not having fun.

What is really missing is the sense itself, of pure joy. People find that they no longer feel an authentic joyfulness in living, despite all the "fun stuff" they have or do. It seems the concrete sets the standards for "how" and "when" and "where" and with "what" to have fun. Many people have a lot of "fun" toys but never use them. This is the case whether rich or poor and regardless of the stage of life they are in.

For many people, the world has taught them how to fit in, including having the proper toys that the world tells us are fun. Maybe a kind of "keeping up with the Joneses." We see other people and their ways of survival, so we copy their ideas of what fun is supposed to be. We stop making choices of our own and allow the worldly pleasures of the ego to give us joy. Our ego cannot handle joy, but who we truly are is all joy.

The only way to see through this charade and get out of this trap is to, first of all, begin viewing "giving" and "receiving" as different aspects of the same thought, especially the giving to, and the receiving from, yourself, just as Mitch Robbins did.

Next is to begin understanding that when you place limits on anything, you impose these limits on everyone else you see. Remember that the Holy Spirit is limitless, and so are you and your brothers/sisters. You must begin to see all others as you see yourself. Spiritual freedom is gained inside of you through the Sonship. Truth is in the Sonship, where your spiritual freedom awaits you.

The truth of the matter is that you *do* realize the body is a loss and will eventually turn to dust. So when you see another as a body apart from you, and separate in his/her own prison cell of a body, you are seeing a sacrifice of both of you. If we are all separate, we are all lost; if all are One, nothing is lost. Every sacrifice you make is reinforcing your belief that you are separate and not at one with your Creator and the Sonship. The ego's purpose of demanding sacrifice is to make the world recede, replaced by only what your body's eye can see, which is the concrete.

The only way to spiritual freedom is to witness truth instead of illusion. We are not separate; but each of us has our role to play as part of the whole Sonship. Without your special function the world has no meaning for you. Your special function can become your treasure house, as rich and limitless as Heaven itself. Therefore, don't be afraid of or embarrassed by your abstract thoughts. This is where you truly exist.

The Holy Spirit's function is to release us from the imprisonment we've made. Now it is your special function to open the door and accept the light the Holy Spirit shines through. To make it easier for you to enter the realm of spiritual freedom, simply ask yourself this question: Can my own function truly be a task apart and separate from His own?

Chapter 17

Correcting the Problems You Think You Have

We all have had our share of problems that make life miserable for us at times. Let's take a look at and try to understand why we don't ask the Holy Spirit to solve all of our problems for us—and why and how we should.

Our problems can appear in many forms, and will do so while the problem lasts. It serves no purpose to try and solve a problem in some special way you dreamed up. It will simply recur, and then recur again, and yet again, until it has been solved for all time to come, after which it will never rise again in any form. Only then will you be released from the problem.

The Holy Spirit is the only means you have for offering you this release from any and all problems you think you have. All of our problems are the same to Him because each one is solved for one, and only one, reason, and through the same approach. The different aspects that need solving do not change, whatever the problem seems to take. This is so because each problem, regardless of the form it seems to take, is always a demand that someone should suffer loss and make sacrifice so that you may gain. This makes it simple for the Holy Spirit to solve them all in the same manner. Separation has taught us our views of gaining and losing. But only when a situation is worked out so nobody loses is the problem actually gone, because it was an error in perception that now has been corrected. It's that simple for the Holy Spirit: He simply changes how you perceive the situation. That's it! Very ingenious, wouldn't you say?

One mistake is not more difficult for the Holy Spirit to bring to the table of truth than is any other. But there is one mistake that causes all of our problems. It is our whole idea that loss is possible and could result in gain for anyone. If this were true, and you could possibly lose in order for someone else to gain, or if someone else could lose for you to gain, then God would be unfair, sin would be real, attack would be justified, and vengeance would be a fair game.

This one mistake in any form has one correction. It's as simple as this: There is no loss. To even think there is, is a mistake in your thinking. You have no problems; you just think you do. Yet, you couldn't think so if you saw them vanish one by one without regard to size, complexity, or place and time, or even any attribute you perceive that makes each one seem different from the rest.

Don't think that the limits you impose on what you see are going to limit God in any way. They can't, because you have His Will to fulfill. There can be no problems for you when you are fulfilling your true function.

Long before my incarceration I thought there was a pile of ongoing problems in my face. I believe these illusory distractions caused me to make wrong decisions that ultimately landed me in prison. But these problems, as I perceived them to be, were merely errors in the way I was traveling along an illusory pathway. Not only was I on the wrong road, but also using the wrong means for getting nowhere. My vision was obscured by the entanglements on the path. The Holy Spirit put up the brick wall where I was forced to make a screeching halt. This was a part of His undoing process, and it continues for me to see.

Yes, of course, I'm here in prison for a while. A physical pit stop along the way. I'm not happy to be here, but I sense joy in the fact that I now understand the process and what is going on. I no longer have any problems. Not only will I be released from prison soon, I have been released from my errors as well.

At this time it is as though I am seeing a track of fallen dominoes standing back up one by one, but in a new, passionate design. I'm beginning to see a path to a purpose, and living it at this moment as I write to you. Things are unfolding one at a time, and the right people are showing up to assist me on my path. I'm seeing this and it is truly amazing.

The miracle of justice can correct all errors. Every problem is simply an error. It does injustice to you, and therefore is not true. The Holy Spirit does not evaluate injustices as great or small, more or less, because they have no properties to Him. They are simply mistakes that are making you suffer, but needlessly. With this knowledge, you can stop crucifying yourself and ask the Holy Spirit to remove the nails and the crown of thorns.

He will not stop to judge whether you are hurting little or large. He makes only one judgment: that you as God's Son must not hurt in any size; and that for you to hurt another is unjust for you. Therefore, your hurt is merely more error that will be corrected. Just ask Him to correct any and all errors, so you may serve your function, which is your free will.

However, a word of caution: Do not believe it is safe to give only some of your mistakes to the Holy Spirit for correction, while you keep others to yourself. You must lay all the cards on the table. Remember that justice is total. There is no such thing as partial justice. If you feel guilty, you are condemning yourself. You cannot only condemn part of yourself. You cannot only fulfill part of your purpose ... just as you do not only have part of a purpose.

God knows that you are innocent. He knows the ego causes you to make errors, and this is why He gave you the Holy Spirit as a part of who you are. This is the means God wants you to travel with, so you can be fully and wholly purposeful.

Each time you keep a problem for yourself to solve, or judge, that is a problem that has no resolution. You are only making it tougher on yourself to heal and for correction of errors to occur. You are denying the miracle of justice.

Like many people, I always saw God as an observer, a judge, keeping track of things I did wrong. This would determine if I would go to Heaven or Hell. I was seeing God as "out there." But when I recognized my true Source better, it seemed to me as though life had been like a bicycle ride, on a tandem bike. I always saw God in the back, a helper to whom I would pray when I needed help pedaling.

Then it hit me, and my position on the bike was corrected. God suggested I get off the bike and get back on again, but this time taking the seat in the back. I was instructed to let the Holy Spirit take the front seat, because He knows the path that God laid out for my purpose. I see the journey ahead much differently now, filled with joy and ambition.

When I had control, I thought I knew the road ahead. I was often fearful and uncertain where I was heading. But when I screeched to a stop at the brick wall, He took the lead, and it's been that way ever since. My prison confinement is part of the route for now and will pass by.

My Guide has taken me on some unbelievable cuts, up mountains and through rocky places at breakneck speed—a path that God has built. I now feel like it's all I can do to hang on, as much of it has looked like madness, especially here in prison. My Guide keeps telling me to "Pedal, pedal."

Sometimes I worry and become anxious, asking, "Where are you taking me?" He just laughs and convinces me to trust. It seems I have forgotten my troublesome and problematic past and have entered into His adventure, which really is mine. He seems to be taking me places and to people I need to meet, even here in prison. I'm receiving gifts that help me. Gifts of healing, acceptance, and joy. I would have to say that acceptance has been my most treasured gift. I know I'm on a journey that is at one with the purpose of all things.

My Guide, the Holy Spirit, has been showing me how to give gifts back, and many times the recipients don't even realize it. I'm finding out that in my giving I continue to receive. My burden does seem light.

It was scary at first, to accept my Guide and allow Him to be first on the tandem bike ride. But I see now that He has the secrets, knowing how to take us around sharp corners and ride over places filled with rocks, roughing it through scary places.

His undoing of my errors has taught me to just keep on pedaling, even in the strangest places, such as where I sit right now while writing this. However, as nasty as my surroundings are at this moment, I do see messages in my view, and they are meaningful.

When I feel tired or fed up, as I often do, He just smiles at me and says, "Keep on pedaling."

Let's take all this into the realm of your true essence by asking yourself two questions: If God is *just*, can there be any problems at all that justice cannot solve? Next, do you believe that some injustices are fair and good—necessary to preserve and protect yourself?

These are the problems that we think are great and cannot be resolved. Isn't this what we are doing when we drop bombs on other lands, but tell ourselves that we try our best to minimize the death toll of the innocent? Isn't this what we did when we took land from the Native Americans, because "If we didn't, someone else would have?" Isn't this what you do when you spank your child and say, "This will hurt me more that it hurts you?"

It seems there are those we want to see suffer loss, and no one we wish to see being preserved from sacrifice entirely. Isn't other peoples' "dirty laundry" what we like to see, especially when it is someone we feel is more successful than us, such as the problems of movie stars that clutter the media? When they are exposed, doesn't this give us a sense of safety?

Consider once again your special function. Your tandem bike ride. One that is given to you to see in your sister her perfect sinlessness—only errors, that's all. Errors are corrected. And do not ask that your brother make sacrifices, because you do not want him to suffer loss. If you can't do this, you are only seeing his body, and therefore must only see your own. If this is so, you are lacking the sight of truth. It is there. You are just holding it back and are afraid. Ask the Holy Spirit to help you "see another way of looking at the world." Just by asking you are willing to see the truth.

What you are doing by asking is calling out for the miracle of justice to heal you, as surely as your brother. The Holy Spirit will not be content until it is received by you and errors are corrected. When you ask this of the Holy Spirit, it means to Him that you are giving yourself for your purpose, and by your giving it, He can ensure that everyone receives it equally.

Now that you have absorbed that truth in you, think how great your own release will be when you are willing to receive correction for all your problems. You will not keep a single problem, because that pain is not part of your function. You will not want it, and will see every little hurt resolved by the Holy Spirit. All of them are little in His sight and are worth no more than just a little sigh before they disappear to be forever undone and unremembered.

What once seemed to be a big problem, a mistake without a remedy, or an affliction without a cure, has been transformed into a Universal Blessing, your purpose in the world. Sacrifice is gone, and in its place is your knowledge and acceptance of the truth.

Chapter 18

Making Room for Oneness

A Course in Miracles asks us to answer this question: "Where all reality has been withdrawn from what was never true, can it be hard to give it up, and choose what must be true?"

What must be true makes no decisions, because it has nothing to choose from. But if truth could decide on any one thing it would be to continue being all that it really is, which is oneness. There are not two or more sides to truth. Oneness is always true, and it has no room for anything else. Trying to understand this can be quite confusing and conflicting in our mind. The ego relies on conflict to make concrete decisions. The concrete will always give us something to choose from, giving us a reason for decision, which can be complicated.

Spiritual freedom is not complicated when all you know is oneness. In oneness there is no conflict. It cannot be complicated because the complexity is gone. To know is merely to accept the truth as all there is in any given matter. Have you ever tried to explain what "the truth" means? You can't explain it. This is the same as oneness, where nothing conflicts. This is why the ego cannot understand it; there is nothing to decide. One is one, truth is truth; that is all there is to it.

The real world is a choice you make to accept what is real. Nothing in between, no "what ifs" or "maybes." The real world is not an outcome. An outcome can only be perceived. Oneness and truth are not separate and have no outcome. It is what it is, always. If all you can ever have knowledge of is oneness and truth, you will undo every illusion you have ever had. Oneness and truth cannot be sacrificed; only illusions can. There truly is no sacrifice when you "let go" of an illusion, because it was never

100

real. If all you are is perfect oneness and truth, you never have a need to sacrifice.

A Course in Miracles goes on to teach us that "Forgiveness in the world is equal to the justice of Heaven." What else could the justice of Heaven be, other than oneness and truth? In this world we associate sin with the word "forgive." We feel that when we forgive, or when we ourselves have been forgiven, that sin is wiped clean.

No individual can forgive unless he believes in sin or believes that he has been forgiven for his own sin. We said that true forgiveness is to look beyond errors caused by illusion made by the ego. In oneness and truth there is no sin; therefore, you cannot sin. Additionally, we must forgive ourselves for believing in the forgiveness of sin we never had or ever will have. What is real holds no sin. Anything that is a part of our dream of separation is not real. Remember, Adam never awakened from his deep sleep and was still dreaming when he listened to the lies of the serpent. The Son of God, or Sonship, has not yet experienced full awakening. Sin is in the dream and not of the dreamer.

By forgiving ourselves in this way we can turn the world of sin into a world of sinless love, with never-ending trust, which is the oneness I am talking about. No sadness, no parting, because everything is totally forgiven, even forgiveness itself. Nothing can be kept separate, not even conflict. In fact, conflict dissolves.

Allow me to describe a conversation a man once had with my friend Connie, the artist I mentioned earlier. This man was very unusual, which is why my memory must have held onto him.

One Saturday morning Connie and I were seated in the bleachers of a Little League ball field, watching her son play baseball. All of a sudden our concentration was interrupted by the booming voice of a tall, portly man who was the grandfather of another player.

"How ya doin', ma'am? Nice to meet ya! The name is O'Malley."

Connie was startled, and I just smiled in mild amusement, as we both looked up at his ruddy face that framed a mouth in perpetual motion. Connie extended her hand as O'Malley's eyes met hers with a stare. He glanced at me with a nod, but it was evident that it was Connie he wanted to talk to.

He slapped his right knee. "I've been seein' ya here for the longest time and I'm wonderin' what kind of life belongs to such a fine-mannered woman. Would ya mind tellin' me about yourself?" As Connie closed her sketchbook, he added, "Ah, I see yer doin' some sketchin'. Can I see 'em?"

She flipped through about ten pages for him to glance at. All the drawings were of her son in various poses around the ball field. O'Malley paused briefly for Connie to give a nod that she did not mind answering a few personal questions. After all, he was friendly. The older man darted out of the starting gate with a full gallop of questions.

"Where'd ya grow up? ... In Ohio on Lake Erie, eh? Sounds nice. Isn't that somethin', Lake Erie. What's the water like there? ... It's cold and wet, eh? Ya must of done some fishin' or sailin'. Ya did? Isn't that somethin'? And did ya ever win a fishin' contest? ... Me neither. I sure like signin' up for 'em, don't you? The tryin's what gives me a charge.

"How 'bout your family? Any brothers or sisters? ... Six! That's great! I'll be, well, isn't that somethin'? Are they still alive? One sister dead! What happened? ... Did the car accident kill anyone else?"

As Connie explained, O'Malley paused and stared out over the ball field. It was a few moments before he spoke again.

"Thank goodness no one else died. How'd ya get over it? ... Oh, you still miss her, and feel it was your fault, eh? ... She was runnin' a grocery trip for ya, was she? I know how it is. I miss my wife that way too. I couldn't get her to the hospital in time. Died right there in my car, she did. Sometimes when I walk into our kitchen, I can still smell her perfume and I can almost see her standin' at the window lookin' out at the yard. There's somethin' real important about bein' able to miss somebody that much, even after they've been gone for years. It kinda makes ya a better person, don't ya think?

"Do ya have yer mum and dad still with ya? … Oh, just yer mum, and she's yer best friend. Well, isn't that somethin'? For Heaven's sake, have ya always had that beautiful smile? I'll bet ya got yerself a sense of humor, too. … That's great! Laughin's the best medicine, I always say. I'll bet yer a handful when yer mad!

"Say, where's yer husband?" (Of course, he smiled and looked over at me.)

"Oh well, not so bad bein' divorced, eh? It sure seems yer a good mom. … Ya think yer a little hard on the boy, do ya? … Well, I guess that's just bein' a good parent and all."

Then O'Malley's questions took an unusual turn. He asked, "Do ya believe in God, eh? … A Christian, isn't that somethin'? What made ya settle on bein' a Christian? … Has religion always been important to ya? … Well, I'll be darned. Isn't that just great!"

On and on O'Malley questioned Connie as she answered. He was spontaneous and unabashed, and he had no pretensions or judgments to make. He was never flustered by a topic or the response Connie gave.

O'Malley had no reservations about finding the truth about Connie. No matter how terrible the facts might seem to be or any of her wrongdoings, he had no inhibitions about uncovering them. He showed no need to label her as sinful or to prove himself an expert. He liked her for what she was, and there was nothing about her past that could change the way he saw her. He was aware of the nature of forgiveness. He had no inclination to even suggest forgiveness to my friend, while simply showing understanding and his knowledge of her true heart.

In this way of being, sin no longer occupies the space in our minds that we made between ourselves and our brothers/sisters. The ego in all of us placed this space in an area next to truth and called it sin. When we shine truth into that space of sin, truth makes it become vacant. As sin, and all other illusions, are cleared from that space, it now becomes a connection or link of brother to brother.

This place where brother to brother connect is the face of Christ, filling in the space where sin is no more. Where you once thought sin existed, arises room for oneness and truth.

Chapter 19

Crossing Over the Bridge to "Now"

A wild and wanton wind one day invaded a peaceful nest where a family of seeds lived. Without invitation the boastful breeze kidnapped the tiniest of the defenseless little kernels and carried it away.

The single seed fell into a strange, alien turf. Here, alone and lost, it rolled across a concrete sidewalk until it was stopped by a dry crack in the barren concrete. Next, an innocent, hapless heel of a boot stepped on that seed, wedging it deep into a crevice. It was trapped. An imprisoned refugee, helpless and hopeless. Discarded and separated from its family, it was alone—an orphan seed clamped tight in a deep, dark canyon.

Then it happened. Trusting in its fate and letting go of the past, deep within the heart of that seed there stirred a strange but miraculous life force. It came to see the sidewalk and the whole world as both its means and purpose for sprouting.

When the first gentle drop of morning mist oozed into that crack in the cement, this small seed welcomed and absorbed the friendly moisture. Little wisps of dust, moved by a gentle breeze, slipped into the crack to blanket the struggling seed, which cried out, "I shall take root and grow regardless of how I got here!"

Softly and silently it sent out microscopic hairy roots that discovered inner crevices in the unlikely environment. There, in miniature hidden caves, the tender tendrils found more moisture, more powdery nourishment, until the seed, swollen with determination, broke wide open and burst forth with a new life. And on a bright sunny morning a blade of grass, green with enthusiasm, popped out of the crack on the sidewalk. Now smiling at the sun, laughing at the rain, waving at the wind, it proudly declared, "Here I am, world! I used your help and made it, regardless of all the mishappenings."

What may seem or feel like the end, most likely indeed is the end. Therefore, welcome it, as it is the end of the past and a step forward into a new dawn. Terminations turn into transitions, which nourish transformations. This is where we find our opportunities for a new inspiration feeding on exciting ambition.

The path we choose in life is far less important than the teacher we choose. There are only two teachers to choose from—the Holy Spirit or the ego—and they point to two different directions. Whether you have realized it or not, you have always been on the path to spiritual freedom. But now you are trying to understand the lessons of your chosen teacher. The path of oneness does lead you to Heaven, which is where you have always been, only you have been in a dream. The dream can only lead to continued dreaming, nightmares, and fears that take you nowhere, while the proper teacher will slowly help you to awaken. If you're still having problems understanding this, it is because all of your trust has been in the wrong teacher. This teacher has directed your focus to your body as who you are, and taught your thinking to be concrete. We must understand that the concrete ends at the graveyard, with our name chiseled into a stone.

Our Creator gave us His Teacher, the Holy Spirit, to replace the one we made that keeps us in the dream of separation. The Holy Spirit does not need to raise conflict, but He does need to replace what needs replacing. His replacement efforts will only take an instant in time, which is the same amount of time you have been dreaming. His efforts will not have an effect on eternity, because nothing can. So simply ask that He do the job.

As you let Him take over as your Teacher, all time that has passed is now gone. Everything now is exactly as it was before you decided on a path to nothingness. Your path to nothingness has been a long and weary journey, and for now you can't even remember what it was like before you started. In the dream, you don't know what it is like to be awake. The dream seems very real. However, you are still the same and unchanged—only now you have a new Teacher Who is guiding you to awakening, rather than deeper into the dream.

There was a tiny tick of time when each of us made the first error and slipped into the dream of separate surroundings. Within that single error stemmed more errors within the dream, and others branched. While these errors were stemming and branching, they also held within them their correction. In that tiny tick of time before we drifted off to dreamland, which is now gone, God gave us a protector. This is our answer.

Your journey continues to answer, and now your new Teacher is showing you Its effects. However, we cannot fully awaken until the world as-one awakens. The ego, our former teacher, wants us to shift back and forth between the past and the present. Much of our time is spent looking at the past as if it were real. But our real, or right-mind views the past as a dream. How many times have you thought, "It all seems like it was a dream?"

Your abstract thoughts receive the Holy Spirit's whispering into your dreaming mind. He helps you to see yourself standing on the bridge between the past and the present. At this position on the bridge a shadow of the past reaches you, but a light of the present shines in your face. Now that this light has flooded your eyes, this is where you exist. It is drawing you over to the present, where you need to stay. The "now" is the only way to awaken.

The illusory habits of mind you still carry with you hear voices in the shadow, but they do not change the laws of time and eternity. They are only echoes of what is past and gone. They could never be your true existence of the here and now.

Once you have crossed over the bridge and entered the real world, there is a second part of the dream or hallucination to confront. It is the belief that time and death are real and have an existence you think you perceive. This terrible illusion was denied for you in the time it took God to give His Answer: the Protector, Whose job it is to help you see the illusion for what it is. You have this help for all time to come and for every circumstance. In other words, the Holy Spirit accompanies you while you dream. You will know that you have crossed the bridge when you can see that time and death only affect your body.

Forgive the past and "let it go," because it is gone. You are no longer on the bridge that connects the two worlds. In fact, the bridge no longer exists. "Now" is where you exist. You may be asking yourself, "How do I know when I am there?" The answer is simple. When you no longer have to think about it.

Chapter 20

God Is the Strength in Which I Trust

Frank and Lorna were kind enough early in my career to be among my first clients, not to mention the referrals they sent me. They were a fun-loving couple and always on the go. Very much in love with each other, they had a close family with three children and a few young grandchildren. They had been married for just over thirty years when I first met them.

Frank thought more of Lorna than anything or anyone else in the world. They were always traveling the country in their motor home and saw much of the USA. Lorna was fighting internal cancer and was undergoing serious chemotherapy treatments. She had just finished a lengthy series, hoping it would be her last. The doctor was going to be in touch with her within a few weeks about her progression.

Lorna said the way she felt was odd. Her body physically was very weak, but she had a strong desire to keep moving, and this, she said, was a source of strength. Rather than sit around and wait to hear from the doctor, the two took off for a much-needed thirty-day excursion in the motor home. Lorna died during the trip. Her body was flown back home, and Frank had to travel back home alone to greet the body and prepare for the funeral.

When Frank purchased a headstone for the cemetery, he had it inscribed: "The light of my life has gone out." Frank was lost for a few years and even told people that he felt as though he was walking in his sleep. He had no desire in him whatsoever.

That was until he met a young lady, ten years younger than he, and fell head over heels in love. He realized he had been mistaken about his first wife being the only person to satisfy his thirst for life. He felt there was something new being added to his purpose for living. He gained the knowledge he was able to fill the void in his life. He realized it was not his decision to meet and fall in love with Ellie.

Frank asked Ellie to marry him, and she accepted, with one simple request. Ellie knew about the inscription on Lorna's headstone and asked that Frank try to change it somehow. So Frank went about looking for someone to either remove or change the wording on the headstone.

When Frank found a man who was able to fix the headstone, he went back to Ellie with the news and the couple went ahead with the wedding. All Frank told Ellie was that he had found another way of looking at everything. When the two came home from their honeymoon, traveling out West in the motor home, they took a ride out to the cemetery.

Ellie was surprised—in a humorous, joyful, and loving way— when she saw that the inscription on the headstone now read: "The light of my life has gone out, but I struck another match."

We have all lost our desire and ambitions at some point in our life, running out of steam when we needed it the most—then feeling more miserable over our loss of purpose or energy, and even more miserable contemplating the effort we see ahead of us just trying to get back on our feet.

You, like me, may have been taught to trust yourself. We've heard it before: "Just tell yourself you can do it" or "You can do anything you set your mind to." And my favorite, "Work a little bit harder and you'll make it." Let's take these loving and well-intended lessons to another level—to the level where our real mind and our real self prevails.

If you are trusting in your own strength, you have every reason to be apprehensive, anxious, fearful, and lonely. What is there in yourself you can predict or control? What is there in you that can be counted on? What is in you that gives you the recognition of the right solution and the guarantee that it will be accomplished?

Your ego-based self can do none of these things. To believe that you can is to put your trust where trust is unwarranted. It is to justify your fear, anxiety, depression, sorrow, and anger. Who can put their faith in weakness and feel safe? On the flip side of the coin, who can put their faith in strength and feel weak?

God is your safety in every circumstance. He is in you, and the Holy Spirit does the communicating. His Voice speaks for Him in all situations, telling you exactly what to do in order to call upon His strength. His protection is guaranteed. There are no exceptions because God has no exceptions, and the Voice that speaks for Him knows all of this.

EXERCISE #2

I hope you have already started a daily routine for Exercise #1, *"There is another way of looking at the world."* Whatever point you have reached in your twenty-one-day daily exercise, you can now incorporate Exercise #2. Or you can always feel free to start over with a new twenty-one days.

Next I want you to reach past your own weakness to your Source of your own real strength. Only you know how to locate it. This will take all the truth that you are about. Go ahead, find it now.

It is now time to add Exercise #2: *"God is the strength in which I trust."*

As you see fit, and in a manner comfortable to you, put Exercises 1 and 2 together.

For example, you can now say, *"There is another way of looking at the world, and I now can see that God is the strength in which I trust."* Try to put a rhythm to this as you start your day and go about your day.

You are now trying to slip past all concerns related to your own sense of inadequacy. You will feel the ego try to nudge you from your resolve by insisting you are still inadequate. But understand it is obvious that any situation that causes you concern is associated with these feelings of inadequacy—otherwise you would believe that you could deal with the situation successfully. It is not by trusting yourself that you will gain confidence. You will come to sense the strength of God in you as successful in all things.

The recognition of your own frailty is a necessary step in the correction of your errors, but it is hardly sufficient to give you the confidence you need, and to which you are entitled. You must also gain an awareness that the confidence in your real strength is fully justified in every respect and in all circumstances.

Now when you practice with Exercises 1 and 2 joined together as one, try to reach deep in your mind to a place of real safety. You will start to recognize that you've reached it if you feel a sense of deep peace and security, however brief it may be. Next, let go of all trivial things that churn and burn on the surface of your mind.

There is a place within you where there is perfect peace. There is a place where nothing is impossible. This is where the strength of God abides within you.

Again, your modified daily exercise is now: *"There is another way of looking at the world, and I now can see that God is the strength in which I trust."*

Chapter 21

A Perceived Antichrist

How often do we look for some outside source to give us strength we think we are lacking? Be it physical or psychological or emotional strength, we feel it is somewhere to be found. Have you ever had the strong urge to make a statement that you know is true, and your own conviction in the matter is burning in your heart, but you still seek additional support that you are unable to attain—and then the subject becomes buried? Such a statement may be of a physical nature, such as proving yourself, or a verbal message you want to give; it really makes no difference. It seems we must always point to the past as a reference for the support we need. Lawyers and judges are good at this when citing past court cases where one ruling weighed over another.

If so many of us have idols that we look to for strength, then how many idols must actually exist in the world today? What is so special about an idol, and what does one truly do for you? Do you really understand where the power lies in an idol? The answers to these questions contain a lot of uncertainty, and our uncertainty is what gives an idol its power. How quick are we to believe the latest news from the gossiper who rules the neighborhood or the office? You know this person—the one who always has the inside scoop on the drama that he or she creates. For that matter, how often do we believe what the newspapers print on the latest scandal? My own court case was a prime example, when I was indicted by the grand jury and portrayed as "being brought to my knees."

An idol is an image of someone or something that we value for what we think it is, in comparison to what we think we are. Idols are constantly replaced—a body, a thing, a place, a situation or circumstance; the news, an object owned or wanted, even a right demanded or achieved. These examples are all the same: something we think gives strength.

Don't let an idol's form deceive you. In some manner we believe an idol can complete our inferiority and make us feel safe in a world perceived as dangerous, filled with forces that threaten our peace of mind. We believe our idols have the power to supply our lacks and give us value we think we cannot attain on our own. When you have an idol, it is your way of enslaving yourself to littleness and to loss. You will try to seek beyond your little self for the strength to raise your head, seen as accomplishment. Perhaps you enslaved yourself so low, you actually did achieve to rise to another level that the world will recognize you for. You thank your idol, and thus have separated yourself from the "losers" in the world from whom you stand apart. But this sort of perceived "gain" is, in reality, further tragic separation from the oneness that is your true self.

An idol is a false impression or a false belief that the ego uses to keep the past alive. It occupies a gap in your mind between the past and the presence of the Christ-Mind in you, which is always in the "now." Its goal is opposite that of the Holy Spirit's bridging of perception to knowledge. An idol strives to build its bridge from past to future with a bypass over the present "now." It doesn't see any benefits to "now," just as it will never understand eternity.

An idol is a wish that is given form and is perceived as real. It is always seen as outside the mind. But it is still only a perceived thought. An idol—the anti-Christ, if you will—is the perception that merely blankets the Christ-Mind in you, like a dark veil that seems to shut off the real you. Have you ever made a sarcastic and judgmental comment, only to immediately say to yourself, "I can't believe I just said that" or "That's not like me?" Or have you ever, in a frightened or insecure moment, told yourself, "What the hell am I afraid of?" This is the Christ-Mind coming through the veil.

The idol works at keeping you in the darkness, and sooner or later or even immediately, the illusion is seen for what it is when the light shines through. Look at it this way: Does a cloud turn off the sun's light, or does it merely obscure the light? No more can a veil vanish the face of Christ. What really is the face of Christ? It is the Wholeness of what you are. It is how you picture yourself when you say, "I can't believe I just said that." Or it can be the strength you picture when you say, "What the hell am I afraid of?" These pictured thoughts of your real strength and your real truth are the face of Christ. It is the thoughts you have of this interlocking chain of oneness and love and truth—your own thoughts and not those of an organization or another individual.

The world of idols in itself is a veil that the ego uses to cover this picture. When the picture—the face of Christ—is covered, it leaves us with dark and fearful questions. We cannot see where our safety lies, so we rely on the idol for direction. An idol is a substitute for what lies under the veil, leaving no room for truth and knowledge. It is the perceived way, where everything that is real is excluded. It is as though a hand is held up in traffic, demanding God to stop for a while so traffic can flow by. Who or what could truly have a voice to make such a demand? We believe our idols are "more than everything," but how can what is not whole and infinite accomplish that? This wholeness we are is Christ, having no enemy and certainly not of physical form. Let's not see Christ as a man or woman, but more so, what *makes* a man or woman.

With this truth known within you, what do you need in an idol? Nothing! You must believe in an idol before it can have power over you, so that it can be feared. This gives it life in your separated and dreaming mind. If truth and fear cannot coexist, then there cannot be any truth to an idol. An idol feeds on fear, and truth will lift the veil where the picture of who you truly are is revealed. Many people live their entire lives knowing the truth of who they are, but never are able to lift the veil due to this fear.

An idol comes to life through beliefs outside yourself, which your ego thinks must be established for you in order to have strength. The ego loves its idols and fights for their survival. When you withdraw these beliefs, the idol dies. This is the anti-Christ, a strange perception that there is power beyond your true knowledge and infinity, a power that can outperform eternity. In this illusory place, a perception was set that an idol takes on a form and can shape the world for its own purposes. This is where we who are timeless come to be made slaves of time, while idols teach us to suffer loss and handle it well, because nothing will last, as in "This too shall pass."

Idols do have one thing right, however: "Nothing" does not last. Where can an idol be? Nowhere! Is it possible there could be gaps in the infinite, a place where time can interrupt eternity? Could there be a place where darkness could put out light? If this is so, an idol must be beyond where God has set all things forever, and has left no room for anything else to be, except His Will. Therefore, nothing and nowhere must be where idols can be found, while God continues to be everything and everywhere.

What then is the purpose of an idol? This is a question that has many answers, and each depends on the individual to whom it is asked. The question tells us that the world believes in idols. Idols are worshipped, and many seek to find the perfect idol for their own circumstances—something "out there" that may give them what they feel is missing in their own reality. Each worshipper of idols harbors hope that his beliefs will give him more than others possess. It must be more, otherwise they seek out a new idol.

It really doesn't matter more of what: more beauty, more intelligence, more wealth, more faith, or even more affliction of pain. More of something is what we "idol" for. But let's not concern ourselves here with the forms this "something" takes. An idol is merely the means for "getting," and this is not God's Will.

God wants you to truly have everything you deserve, because you are an integral part of the Sonship, His only Son, who needs to have everything in order to fulfill His purpose. There is no idol that could ever intrude with "more." The Holy Spirit does all the "getting" for your purpose, and this means that He will make sure you have everything you want. Your wants are your needs that are necessary for you to have the peace of maintaining your place in the Atonement. Remember, I am talking here about "your" wants, not the ego's. What you want is the will of the Sonship, which is, as well, the Will of God.

If having everything you want is within you, why would you want an idol that would make you lesser in order to give you more? This is the same as taking two steps backward, and then one step forward. God is all that there is. When your idol dies, the Creator of everything remains forever with you as His Idea. If you are His Idea, then you are of Him, and no idol can establish you as more than God.

Therefore, what is an anti-Christ? It is a perception that makes fantasy believable. It is the *perception* that sees it acceptable to target bombings so they minimize the death toll of the innocent. It is the same *perception* that sentences a man to prison for political gain, or that finds one's neighbors inferior, or that claims privilege at others' expense. It is the perception that makes up its own truths.

However, there is no need to worry that an idol could ever take the real you to that level, because you would never be content with being less than God.

PART IV

THE REALIZATION OF TRUTH,
MAKING NO ROOM FOR ILLUSION

Chapter 22

Sickness as an Illusion

The peaceful and more relaxed way you see the world is a sign that you are getting to know the real world through yourself. I liken this process to how I would feel whenever I left my home in Ohio and got on the highway to drive to sunny Florida. My perception of the trip would change little by little, the closer I got to the Florida line. This was particularly evident in the wintertime, when I left snow and gray skies, gradually arriving to abundant sunshine. Similarly, by now you should be noticing the healing process within yourself that we discussed early on. You should by now be realizing a feeling of not being alone. The laws of healing must be understood so this feeling can gradually strengthen as you continue to spend time in your right-mind. As your transition becomes more securely set in the real world, you will experience healing continuously on the spiritual path.

Let's go over a few necessary principles I have learned, arranged in a way that summarizes all that must occur for you to experience healing.

A key healing principle is to be aware that all sickness stems from your belief in separation. Only when you are able to deny separation from the One Thought of God does sickness not only go away, but will never come about. It is gone because the idea that brought it on has been healed and replaced by sanity. What is sanity? All that is true. Sickness and sin are seen as consequence and cause in a relationship that your ego-based thinking keeps hidden and uses for its own illusory reasoning. Take, for example, a fever and sniffles—seen as a consequence—caught by babysitting the neighbor's children—seen as cause.

Here in prison we are expected to get colds and flulike symptoms on a regular basis. The prison system does a grand job of giving us these "cold" hard facts to process in our belief system. This is due to the fact that we literally live within thirty inches of one another, where germs and bacteria have a prime breeding ground. Of course regular hand-washing and personal hygiene are measures of precaution, but there simply is no stopping the spread of such infections.

There are always certain inmates who give no regard whatsoever to their own personal hygiene. Some men literally never take a shower and are often forced into segregation, where an "institutional cleansing" can be conducted. No individual, regardless of educational background or social status, wants to have others living in their face, let alone be exposed to the coughing, sneezing, and other bodily functions taking place.

Once, when I came down with a bronchial infection, I immediately started scolding myself for not taking better care, and next started blaming other inmates, as well as the living conditions. This caused me to be quite upset and anxious, and I decided to sign up for "sick call," where the proper antibiotics were prescribed.

My body was suffering from this condition and was also consuming my real self as a part of this illness. I was allowing my mind to see myself as ruled by the virus—as if the virus had power over me. My mind was seeing the virus as evil and demanding and in charge, and I therefore believed I had to fight this thing off. Ironically, this only made it more alive, when in reality I was separating more of my mind from its true Source and engaging in more wrong-minded, or ego-based, fragmentation. I was seeing the virus as my source, or at best an unwanted violator—not to mention my constant hacking and sneezing and fever telling me what was in control. When I allowed blame to set in toward the other inmates, as well as the state prison system for its overcrowded conditions, I used this blame as a defense against the insanity I was experiencing.

Finally I realized I needed to atone with my *true Source*, leaving the virus where it was—in my body—to run its natural course. I found that when I talked to it and faced it head on, letting it understand that in no way was it going to govern who I am, my right-mindedness stood by and merely watched it leave town— just like the sheriff in an old western movie escorting the bad guys to the town's boundary line. To atone here means to undo any separated thought from the Oneness of God. My own ego-based thought was making an illusion out of the virus and building additional ego-based defenses. This defensive ego-based thought thrives on making us feel it necessary to experience loss or sacrifice in order to win battles against enemies—the "other." Our typical response is usually a call "out" to God to please get rid of this nasty illness. The emphasis always seems to be: "I am sick."

When we atone back to our Source we are simply remembering that we are not an idea of our "sick body." We are the Idea of God, which means that this Idea, which is of Oneness, cannot include illness. When you ask the Holy Spirit to direct your awareness back to right-minded thinking, then a connectedness to this Oneness can be felt. You, as an integral part of the whole Sonship, are the Idea of God. In this One single Thought, Ideas are only of your free will, and your free will does not involve sickness.

Is this to say we should not take a prescribed medication, such as the antibiotics? Of course not; the medications can be seen as the gun in the sheriff's hand as he escorts the bad guys out of town. The body can often be heavily influenced by wrong-mindedness, and the medications are simply aiding the body with the physical means necessary to move the ailment along its natural path. Remember, the body is all about the use of time.

The Holy Spirit uses time as well, however, when right-mindedness rushes in to fill the gaps left by the fragmenting ego, as we discussed in detail earlier. When your body is sick it's just a matter of understanding this, which will allow the healing to continue through the right-mind and its perception. While we are occupying our body here on Earth, healing is constantly ongoing, because the ego is constantly fragmenting. The question for you is: Where is the balance of your split-mind in the ratio of wrong-minded to right-minded perception? Which perception is in control, you or the ego? Remember, you made the ego, but it is not who or what you are.

Of course, there are the all-too-sad more tragic illnesses, which are also due to the mind's separate state, where deterioration of the body begins. But the body is always either growing or deteriorating. The body will eventually turn to dust, and this fact causes us fear. Why? Because we will be without the ego, and being afraid is of the ego. So it is really not you that is in fear, it is the ego, a thing you made. Instead, if you can understand and gain a "feeling realization" that it is the body that will eventually branch off and wither away from who you are, then you will not fear, in the knowing that you will live on where there is no sickness, and never was. You are not about sickness, but your ego-based thought is. This is where the fear comes from: the guilt you feel for not accepting and realizing who you truly are.

The guilt that you have been living with all along is asking to be punished, and its request is granted, as well as the sickness. But in truth this is not so, because the shadows you feel touching you from your past do not really exist. We carry guilt from the past with us as if it were our baggage. We think this baggage is who we are. The baggage is the illusion we made and we call it sin, thereby labeling ourselves as sinners.

Think about it. You perceive how you want to see things, making perception a wish fulfilled. You continually change, trying to keep up with the changeless knowledge you desperately search for.

But you don't have to make any efforts hunting for it. It is in you, and always has been and always will be. It's called unalterable, never-ending truth. Just simply start seeing truth in everything, and you will have no problem living by it, because it is you. What is there truly to fear in the fact that your body will one day turn to dust? What you perceive fearfully can take on many forms, but has no true meaning. Nonetheless it is a perception, and is a step on the bridge to knowledge.

Once you can welcome the bridge from perception over to truth, you will see the senselessness in your fears. All journeys start with a single step, and your journey to truth starts with the step of making a perception; whether it is wrong-minded or right-minded, it is a step. If it is wrong-minded, merely by your asking the Holy Spirit will bridge that gap over to right-mindedness. Truth stands as one and cannot intrude on your perceptions, but it can welcome your questions to open arms as He answers.

Perception's laws are opposite to truth, and what is of knowledge can only be what is true. God does give answer to the world of sickness, which applies to all forms. God's answer is eternal, although it works in time where it is needed. But because it is of God, the laws of time do not affect its workings. His answer is in this world, but not only in this world. It is where all reality must be, in ideas, which are of thought and remain in thought.

How could it be that scientists recently found DNA from fossils of extinct flies, weevils, spiders, and lizards that lived 120 to 135 million years ago? They were fossilized for millions of years in a sticky resin from trees that hardened with time. In this DNA scientists are now able to activate a single cell to help make major breakthroughs.

Another team of researchers has developed a new experimental treatment for lymphatic cancer. The antibodies were attached to radioactive iodine and injected into the bloodstream to kill cancerous cells. Additionally, a DNA link in genes of mice has been proven to prevent stages of muscular dystrophy. These genes are now being put into humans.

Dr. Albert Sabin, the developer of the oral vaccine for polio in the 1950s, died in 1994 at the age of eighty-six. To this day, children around the world continue to be vaccinated against this once-common disease.

Ideas do not leave the thought of their source, and the effects only seem to be separate from them. Ideas are of the mind, the One Mind. What is extended out and seems to be external to the mind, is not outside at all. It is merely an effect of what is still in the mind and has not left God.

God's answer, which is cause, comes through wherever you hold your beliefs in sin because this is where the effects of your illusory sins are undone by the Holy Spirit. For example, for years I had been living under the tyranny of the instruction to "Judge not"—and failing. Much of my judgment of others was a projection of my own fears. But then I read of the Dalai Lama's description of "inner disarmament." Somehow the concept of "disarmament" helped me to lay down my defensive armory of criticism and judgment of others. Of course I still have judgments, but I now try to accept even my judgments without judging them. At a pace right for me, I moved beyond repression and self-criticism to something more skillful. I've somehow been taught the difference between recoiling from feelings and opening to them, and now I am apt to be more curious than fearful.

In other words, the Holy Spirit gets rid of what is not real. Real cause is of God, as are its effects, and the Holy Spirit in you makes corrections to your illusions so you will realize the real effects. Much like truth and knowledge, cause and effect are one and not separate.

We must learn to reverse perception's laws, because we made them to be the reverse of the laws of truth. Somewhere along the line we seem to have made a law that equates perception with knowledge. Thus, since perceptions change, we made changeable truths. But the laws of truth will forever be true and cannot ever be changed or reversed. We do see this and we do know it, but we continue to perceive, thus making our own truths, therefore not living by our own true knowledge, which is truth.

This is what the Holy Spirit corrects, in order that you may live God's Will. What exactly is God's Will? His Will is that you have everything you truly want, in order that you can meet the need to carry out your purpose. Your purpose is your free will, which gives you your place in the Atonement.

Chapter 23

Seeing through Illusion

When I was growing up with four sisters and one brother, all younger than me, we had many toys and games around the house. My sister Jolyn, having had a fetish for monkeys, introduced me to the well-known book, *Curious George*. Do you know the story of Curious George and his activities?

The book is about a monkey who touches things, picks up anything that is not nailed down, opens doors, plays with telephones, explores the back of trucks before they take off … and gets himself into all kinds of monkey business. Nothing can escape the notice of this little monkey. Children love Curious George because he is so much like them.

The human race would never have made any progress in understanding itself and the world if we had not been aware of the possibilities in the people around us, beyond what the world dictates. It is a shame we have to tell a child in a store not to touch, or direct her attention to homework when she would rather play and learn more about herself on her own.

Learning to discipline your mind and focus your thoughts is a part of growing, but that does not mean your awareness of the whole world should be squeezed out entirely. We must preserve our impulse to explore, probe, to notice things and to be aware of everything. Rather than accept everything you see, allow yourself to notice. Ask questions. Find out how things work and why they are here instead of there. Try to discover for yourself why roses are red and the sky is blue. Look for colors and beauty, and prepare to be surprised.

Surprise makes us pause and give awe a chance to happen. To be open to awe, we must open up to surprise. Most of us like the idea of surprise, and it is an important part of experiencing awe, which helps us to see directly through illusion.

A Course in Miracles makes the statement that "No illusion has any truth in it." Every day we face illusion, and it's impossible that one illusion may justify itself to truth more than any other. But, though much of the time we value some illusions more than others, this cannot help truth in any manner with our healing. The Holy Spirit cannot make correction for illusion to illusion, only for illusion to truth. The illusion is not real, and when the Holy Spirit helps you make the shift over to right-mindedness, you can see that without illusion, all that is left is truth.

Yet we try our best to make it appear that some illusions are more true than others, which clearly gives us an untrue meaning to what really is the truth. When we assign categories we do show a preference to our illusions, but this cannot be reality. Truth does not have categories and cannot be stacked up and prioritized. Illusions are illusions and are not of God. Not one is more important than another. Because illusions are not true, they have no cause, and therefore can have no effects. Jesus told us about how illusions are built on sand and have no foundation for truth.

A Course in Miracles goes on to say that "Sin is not error, for it goes beyond correction to impossibility."

The world has convinced us that sin is real, and this belief is what makes errors seem to be beyond the hope of healing, thereby giving us grounds for the belief in hell. If hell is real, then it must be true because what is real is also true. If hell really is true, then how could Heaven be the opposite to hell, when truth has no opposites? Heaven most certainly is true, and if hell were also true, wouldn't this make eternity forever split in two? If this is so, and eternity is split, this would mean God's Will is also split in two, and all of creation as well.

Even worse, this would have God opposing and doubting Himself, which would create laws of opposing powers. This would entail God having attack thoughts. This would make Him proclaim sin as a threat to His reality and bring love to the door of vengeance for assistance. Is this an insane picture or what? Yes, it is! And this is what has been going on in our illusory thought process since time began. We have built organizations around these manmade beliefs called religions, and this is why we fear God.

Nothing can give meaning where there is no meaning. Truth needs no defense to make itself true. Illusions have no witnesses and no effects. There is no hell, and there is no sin. If you look at hell and sin as real, then you have been deceived. Forgiveness is the only function there is to rid yourself of this illusion. Yes, that is right. Forgive yourself for your belief in sin and hell. Why? Because the rage and despair you bring on are responses to illusions. But this anger is over nothing, because isn't illusion nothing? The real truth is that you can actually increase the frequency and intensify a response to truth called joy in your life. This joy you produce is the response to your forgiveness of rage and despair. Joy is what you are.

Just like rage and despair, the response of joy can be an external, as well as an internal, cue to make a change in someone else's illusory thought process. The greater our identification with that person's experience, the greater the elation. A child's achievements in school when she thought she did poorly, or a friend's marriage when he thought love was hopeless, or the birth of a healthy baby are mutually joyful moments.

At age seven my oldest daughter Erin was determined to learn how to ride a bicycle. I purchased the bike as a surprise for her birthday. A few other adults, including her overprotective mother, suggested to Erin that she was too young and should wait one more year before learning to ride the bike.

I was the culprit who convinced her she could do it now and did not need to wait till the next year. She bravely positioned herself up and onto that bike without training wheels, as I held it steady and upright. When I asked her if she was ready, and with her permission, I gave the bike a tiny push down a slight slope as she pedaled away, shouting out with elation to the world, "I'm doing it, Dad, I'm doing it, I'm riding a bike all by myself!" I was elated as well, and she proved to everyone and herself that she was not too young to ride a bicycle.

I felt a glow, a rush, and a thrill that I cannot explain, but I am sure you understand. I don't know who was more thrilled, her or me, as she smiled proudly, cheekbone to cheekbone, and sporting those two missing front baby teeth. The thought of this memory is still a hefty joy many years later.

It is possible that you don't see the role of forgiveness in ending all the beliefs that bring on anxiety and guilt. Sins are beliefs that you impose on yourself and on others. How is this? Because they limit you to time and place, separate from your brother, and create space between you. Please keep in mind once again, when I speak of you, him, or me, I'm not talking about the body. The space you put between your brothers as a separation is symbolized in your perception by a body clearly separate. This image, then, represents your wish to be apart and separate.

Forgiveness will take away what stands between your brother and yourself. It is the wish that you be joined with him, and not apart, as you both see the effects of oneness. We call this a "wish" because you are still concerned with choices and have not yet reached beyond the world of choice entirely; but that's okay for now.

The very fact that you recognize this means you are gradually moving beyond the need to make choices. You are growing spiritually. Your wish is in line with the state of Heaven and God's Will, which is your own free will, and your purpose while here on Earth.

So relax, and know that you are moving in the proper direction along the path. If, for now, you fall short of giving your full true essence, your wish for guidance does remove the obstacles you once placed on this path between you and Heaven. You are now recognizing where and what you are, seeing time as not being an interference, and seeing these facts of truth as unchanged. Whether you realize it or not, by accepting this truth of who you are, you are allowing illusions to slowly fade away. The ego doesn't like it, but you can deal with that.

Chapter 24

Be Careful What You Wish For

I can remember one clear, starry night as a boy, when my grandfather and I stood in the side yard to his old two-story home, analyzing the Big Dipper. I asked him, "Do you think someday I'll be able to reach up and touch one of those stars?" My grandfather answered, "You don't have to wait till you're bigger; you're already touching them." With quizzical wonder and my head pointed upward, I responded, "Aw, no way, Grandpa. How could that ever be?" He tapped his index finger against my chest and answered, "Son, those stars are in your heart. That's why you're able to see 'em."

For no other reason than control, the ego, our false sense of self, perceives salvation as something waiting for us down the road. We see it as some future event to prepare for. Could it be the ego wants eminent domain over our time in this world? Yes, the ego wants your time in order to exist, and this is why time concerns you. The continuous search for salvation seems to be on a path the ego directs, where "one day" we will have our home with salvation waiting. Along the journey the ego tells us we must do some of "this" and much of "that," usually on our knees, in order that we may be saved. This is a price we must pay, the ego tells us.

What is wrong with the world's outlook today? Such questions are bound to arise in thinking minds when we ask a simple question: What are we looking to be saved from? However, often the answers given to this simple question are widely varied and never completely honest. The crux of the matter lies in the need today to dig religion from its ancient and narrow dark vault and let the spirit of present-day humankind shine out in honest glory.

Let me share a story about my old friend Willie, the seventy-eight-year-old all-American grandfather I mentioned earlier, who has figured out what the young inmates want. Not only has Willie found safety here in prison, but also his salvation. Willie enjoys watching and listening to the prison choir of fifteen or so inmates who practice each Saturday morning. He noticed that each member of the choir could use some sort of a folder to keep their sheet music organized. At his own expense, Willie purchased through the commissary pocket folders for each member of the choir. At the next Saturday morning practice, Willie surprised each member with his own pocket folder. The men were grateful for his thoughtful gift and welcomed Willie to attend any future choir practices he would like.

All of the members of the choir looked at Willie as a giving and caring grandfather type, and the word got around quickly. In a conversation I had with Willie about his kind act, he told me this was not why he went to the effort to buy the folders. He said to me in a humorous way, "Jim, the only reason I bought the folders for those guys was to get them to like me." He continued chuckling, trusting that I would keep the secret. Was he honest or what? Yes, of course he was—with himself.

For one thing, as the ego tries to lead us to salvation it seems to be fearful of the fact that salvation is already complete and perfect and is nowhere to be found down the road. It is here and now, and always "now" is where your salvation sits for you. It is your true essence that knows what is true and what is not true. Just as with Willie, who accepted within himself why he really bought the pocket folders, regardless what the choir members thought. He had the knowledge that he couldn't fool himself. His true essence was accepted by himself, and this is his salvation.

Salvation is the little smiles you can see within yourself, along with a wink and a nod to your brother, showing your mutual preference for joy over the world that death and wretchedness seem to rule. It is the understanding that you are not separate and that your will and God's Will are one. Somewhere along the line, the world started teaching you how to paint your portrait using its chosen colors and brushstrokes. Your function, as well as God's Will, is to use your own freely chosen colors, perfecting your masterpiece. This is the spirit in you, enabling you to touch the stars.

To be spiritual-minded needs no special time, place, or circumstance. It is not concerned with anything out of your ordinary daily routine. It is just a simple mental attitude toward lasting value, changing circumstances, and avoidable eventualities, as well as accepting the inevitable.

A mighty surge of true spirituality is catching on and will sweep over the entire planet. Your true colors have no meaning in the ego-based world and are not separate from God. Why do you think He gave us His Holy Spirit? To keep what has no meaning out, and only what is real a part of your masterpiece. When you feel off-track or out of sync, just ask that He readjust your way of seeing the world. This only needs to take a few minutes.

You can never ask too often or for too much. But you can ask for too little. With that said, would you sacrifice your true identity with everything, to paint your portrait with "paint by numbers," in order to get a sure little treasure? You won't be able to do this without a sense of loss, isolation, and loneliness. This would always be your only treasure, because you are afraid of what you really want. Think about it. Is fear and incompleteness the treasure you really desire? Can forever wondering "What could have been?" be what you want? Or are you lost and don't know what you want?

There is no more ready means by which to outline your inner self than through honesty. Honesty with your brother is the beginning step. This giving of your honesty must, then, be real, if it is being given away; therefore, you cannot help but have honesty from inside yourself. This will assure there is no hypocrite abiding in you.

Hypocrisy is a million-headed cobra, with a million-dollar budget supporting its million-dollar structures. Today there are so-called saints in the world who tell people to be honest; yet they themselves are deeply involved in dishonesty. Infinite honesty is one of the aspects of your true essence. All you have to do is use it. What are you afraid of? Honesty is the leading light on the inner pathway, and one of the most effective means for healing.

Let us take a look at the error we all face so it can be corrected and not protected. When we believe in sin, we believe that attack in any form takes place outside the mind where the belief arose. This proves that we view ideas as leaving their source. We are thus thinking of the world and ourselves in a physical and material way. Nothing takes place outside the mind; this is why sin is unreal. Remember, only illusion takes place outside the mind—and illusion is not real.

Try to look at it this way: If you give away a material possession, such as a bicycle, the bike is no longer in your possession, no longer a part of you. But if you give away an idea, others can use it and it is still with you. It will always be "your" idea.

Your error lies in the fact that you are still seeing yourself in a material or physical sense, and so you see effects as separate or outside and away from their Source, your Creator. You still have this "magic wand" belief that God makes things happen outside of Himself and Heaven. We see His creations as outside of Heaven's gate. But as you know, anything that is kept separate can never join. Just as the idea you gave away never really separated from you. It will always be your idea. With this understanding, can you now see more clearly that you are the *Idea of God*?

God's Will is that you begin realizing what has always been true is true, and has never been false. I mean, He created you as part of Him, and not separate. God is Thought, and so must you be thought. This must be forever true because ideas do not leave their source. We are the Idea of God, not separate from our Source.

With that understood, let's take a look at Creation's Law: Each idea the mind conceives only adds to its abundance, and never takes away. However, this is as true of what you idly "wish" for as what you truly will. This is why there is something to the old adage, "Be careful what you wish for." You can deceive yourself.

The mind can wish for something and truly be deceiving itself. In this case, you not only sense this, but you cannot be what is not your true color. Therefore, when you think you believe that ideas do separate from their source, you are inviting illusion to be true, without success. The illusions you make yourself see as true continue to make more illusions, driven by illusory goals that you think, or want to think, are true. This goes back to what we talked about earlier, when we decide to make our own truths. Never will success be possible at trying to deceive yourself, because you would be deceiving God.

Your free will must be performed without worrying about consequences, regardless of success or failure. The work you do in this spirit, and with this understanding, yields inevitable results.

Through the joy in the activities of your spiritual way, humanity will move gradually into a new life of abiding peace and dynamic harmony, unconquerable faith, unfading bliss, immortal sweetness, and incorruptible purity. Wouldn't you agree that this is creating love and infinite understanding?

Chapter 25

Seeing in the Here and Now

Between the time when we forgive and the time when we actually feel as though we can trust, we seem to insert an interval. We are taught to forgive, followed by allowing a period of time to do its work. What could this "work" possibly be, that this interval of time is intended to inspire? In reality, all it is doing is enforcing our feeling that there is still something we need to withhold from our brother; we maintain the space that keeps us separate.

From this perception, you cannot conceive of gaining the peace or freedom you were taught that forgiveness will give you. Therefore, there is no gain, and the interval you think lies between the giving and receiving is experienced as a feeling of sacrifice and suffering, due to the anxiety that was built. It can look like this: "If I do this favor for her now, how long will it be till she reciprocates, if at all?" This ego-based thought process has us seeing a hopeful or an eventual salvation rather than immediate results. We are trading a perceived loss for a perceived gain some time in the unspecified future.

Let's back up a moment and look at what *A Course in Miracles* tells us. "Time and space are an illusion which takes different forms." We see the time as a possible "cooling off" period, or a time to "gather one's thoughts," and then, when time comes in closer, we start to see it as space. The thinking seems to be, "I'm okay with her, but I just need a little space." The space and time are seen as physical, which is all they both can be—but we think they are real and necessary in order to have a relationship.

The distance we feel that must be kept between us is perceived as time and keeps us external to one another. This makes real trust impossible. We don't believe total trust can solve a problem, because fear is occupying the space we think we need.

Think about this: Will our nation, which is seen as the leader in the "free" world, ever trust so-called volatile countries to put down their nuclear weapons, as well as their research? This leads us to think it's a little safer to be more watchful over our own interests, seen as separate. Additionally, isn't this really the way we want it to be? It seems as though we feel we want or need this fear in order that we may feel strength.

When this happens, it is a trap, and you will never see salvation unless you can bring the idea of salvation out of the future, which is impossible. You will always be living for future gain and never see it as immediate if you don't start perceiving it, and thus will be afraid to ever have true salvation. Remember, perception will lead to knowledge. If you accept this trap, you will always believe the risk of forgiveness is too great for effects that you may never see. This is how the ego keeps you from trusting in Cause—which is God, by making you fear Its effects.

We said that cause and effect are one and not separate. Who put the space or time between cause and effect? Is not time and space the ego's most-used weapon for defense? Salvation instantly wipes out this space you still see between you and allows you to become at one. What is this salvation I'm talking about here? It is the feeling of not having to protect your fear of oneness. Thus, you don't project this fear out through time—as in, "How long will it take to receive my end of the bargain?" In reality, as *A Course in Miracles* goes on to teach us, "Future loss is not your fear, but present joining is your dread."

The plans we lay out for safety are always for the future, where there is no cause. If there is no cause, how can there ever be effects to plan for? There is no purpose given yet.

I mentioned earlier that humankind has been making the same mistakes over and over again, since the symbolic Garden of Eden. We still continue to plan with "just in case this were to happen" in mind. Don't get me wrong here, as planning is important with the right state of mind. But we get too concerned about events that may occur from our predictions of a cause that never was and too busy planning for effects that will result from past effects and past perceptions, usually wrong-minded.

Consider this: We build more new and improved bombs to defend ourselves against the world, because we perceive that "they" might be building newer bombs that will outperform our bombs. What if the United States of America, the most powerful country on the planet, one day said to the entire world, "We quit, and we will no longer produce a single bomb or weapon of any kind. In fact, we have destroyed our stockpiles."

What would *cause* us to do such a thing? Remember, cause is of God, and He would not cause us to build bombs. But He would cause us to find peace, by stopping the bombs. Cause, in this sense, is the rainstorm; its effect is a peaceful green meadow.

With that said, a cause that never was becomes the illusion bringing on effects, to only bring on more effects. This is why history repeats itself time and again. We make belief in sin arising from an illusory cause. This is symbolized by the apple that Eve bit into, giving her illusory, wrong-minded thinking.

How many starving and homeless people are there in this world, and how many could be fed and sheltered and rehabilitated with the money being used to build bombs? If we ceased building bombs and world hunger came to an end, this would be an effect divinely intended. Once again, I ask you, where is the illusion?

Yet, only here and now can any cause exist. Do you see correction needed here? The process of correction takes no time at all. Rather, it is the acceptance that this process is indeed necessary that can take forever.

When disagreements happen between individuals and even nations, there is a change in purpose the Holy Spirit is bringing to the relationship due to a certain cause. That's all it is; and this brings on new effects that will be seen. They can be looked at now by your true essence or true colors, or you can decide to wait till they unfold and see them in time and with fear. Likewise, you can hope and pray that one day the hungry of the world will be fed, or you can help move along the acceptance movement, now. Or you can fret over waiting till your neighbor pays you back, or you can be content with your act of giving, regardless of reciprocation. These are the effects that came out of a cause that are available here and now, not someday.

We've been raised to believe that everything that comes from God brings good. This is so. But often, doesn't it seem to not be so? Isn't good in the form of disaster now difficult to see? For example, is it good when Mother Nature takes a wrecking ball to her realm in the form of a level-eight earthquake in a populated area? Or is there good in the pain of a seven-year-old child whose parents were suddenly killed? Where is the good in all of this?

Why should we try to see the good in evil's form? Its cause is apparent—so why are we not seeing its good effects? Why in the future? We are taught to be content with "reasoning" to ourselves that we don't understand it now, but will someday. Then, we are told, the meaning will be clear.

This is not reason; this is unjust, and clearly hints at punishment until the time of liberation is at hand. But given a change of purpose for the good, there is no reason to see an interval of space or time when disaster strikes as "good" someday. Hmm, what do I mean? Okay, allow me to explain: When we see things in the form of pain, this becomes a sacrifice of "now," which could not be a cost the Holy Spirit would take. He gives without cost at all. Then what is a disaster all about? Why is there tragedy?

Let me add that I have encountered great difficulty with this kind of question, which led me to much spiritual pondering. I went through lengthy times wondering, but never doubting my own faith. That, for me, is too deeply rooted. *A Course in Miracles* merely gave these deep roots of mine freedom. The freedom to feel good about "my way" or "my faith." However, I wondered why I couldn't complete the connection through my own rational thinking. Why couldn't I reason my way all the way through and figure this out?

That's when I realized my real error and what has always been my big hang-up: my pride in the idea that I could accomplish anything on my own if I set my mind to it. I could not imagine there could be something I could not figure out. Then one day the answer hit me like a lightning bolt in the heart. Could this be it, could this be what cause and effect really is about? I'm certainly feeling an effect!

Then I stumbled into some writings by the French philosopher Blaise Pascal, arguing that God has given us just enough light so that we can understand and just enough darkness or obscurity to deny the truth, if we wish. That was it! Of course, God cannot reveal Himself or His reason for cause, in a rational or irrefutable manner. He would be violating the most fundamental universal law there is.

Remember, we are that universal law that is the Idea of God, and He has given us just enough light to see by, but not enough to eliminate the need to see with eyes of faith. The ego tells us that we should have God on our terms and in our own understanding of the way the world should be.

When reciprocation is finally received, it's not in the future or in future happiness. It is being received now. So let's not be content with future happiness; rather, let us always be living in the here and now. This is where the effects for spiritual freedom truly are. Spiritual freedom or Heaven has no meaning in the future, and there are no rewards. Why else was the symbolic "Tree of

Knowledge" forbidden? This answer is simple, in that there is no future to have knowledge about.

If you are always a prisoner of the future, where then is your freedom? It is always at some future event, just as the promise of salvation. Why should we wait until our body dies to have eternal freedom? Delay is senseless, and so is the reasoning that would tell us that present *cause* must reveal its *effects*.

Therefore, let's not look to time, but rather the tiny space between you and me, so that we might be delivered from it. But don't let it be disguised as time, because this deliverance can only happen here and now.

Chapter 26

God Is My Source—I Cannot See Apart from Him

I hope you are making progress and remain committed to your daily exercise, as you discover that "There is another way of looking at the world." The new look at the world you are gaining should be bringing you closer to finding that perception is not an attribute of God—but if used right, perception can be a path to know Him, which is the realm of knowledge.

Yet He has given us His Holy Spirit as the mediator between perception and knowledge. Without this link with God, perception would have replaced knowledge forever in our mind. With this link to God, our perception will become so changed and purified that it will lead to knowledge. That is the function of perception as the Holy Spirit uses it. Therefore, this perception He uses will link up in truth.

EXERCISE #3

Without interrupting the routine you have set in your daily exercise, at random throughout your day, remind yourself that you cannot see apart from God, because you will never be apart from Him. All of your thoughts throughout the day, when you are "looking at the world in another way," are of Him. Whatever you think, you are doing so with His Mind. If vision is real—and it is real to the extent to which it shares the Holy Spirit's purpose— then you cannot see apart from Him.

To remind yourself of this, simply think or say to yourself as often as you can, and without disrupting your main exercise, these words:

God is my source. I cannot see apart from Him.

If a particular object comes into your awareness, such as a chair or table, then use it in your thoughts as:

God is my source. I cannot see this chair apart from Him.

If there is a particular problem in your day—say your car payment is late or your spouse is grouchy—you can use this in your thoughts as well:

God is my source. I cannot see my wife's grouchiness as reality, because it's not truly of her. We share the same Source.

Don't be too concerned with making a formal ritual of this. Just take a few moments to put this into your thinking each and every day. You will be encouraged when you start seeing your wrong-minded thoughts shifting over to more right-minded thoughts. This will help you to start realizing that *"There is another way of looking at the world."* Even with your grouchy spouse.

Chapter 27

Being a Real Seeker of Spiritual Freedom

Did you ever stop to think how holy you are when the Voice for God within you calls on a brother, or when you see his holiness in the voice that answers your call? How many times have you seen the "different side" to an individual whom others have condemned? What would happen if you opened the door to allow trust to pour into you and outward toward this person? That "different side" that others could not see in him, but that you can see, is the Christ within you both. Or we can simply call this whole picture "the face of Christ." Even your reactions to this loving "other" or "different" side is the Sonship, driven by the Thought of Christ.

The understanding of God, which the average person accepts through belief or reasoning, is so far removed from true understanding that it cannot be called inner knowledge, because it is perceived as "out there." True knowledge does not consist of the constructions or perception of beliefs passed on to us by society. It can only be obtained by ripened experience—not necessarily age—that increases gradually, along with increased clarity. True knowledge grows, or "ripens," inside of you, becoming more real as you participate in only, and nothing other than, pure truth until there is no more to absorb, but it only flows.

The devotional rituals followed in religions do not lead you to true inner travel, which constitutes a true journey, because for the most part they are mechanical observations, barren of the redeeming experience of actually feeling divine love. Therefore, the struggle most always seems to be: What really is divinity?

Now I am not trying to tell you to leave your religion, which surely can be a good foundation for understanding faith—just as mine was for me. The "ups and downs" and "ins and outs" that you experience within the congregation of your place of worship are valuable lessons.

In my early days of *ACIM*, as I struggled through the obscuring fog of mental and emotional tension, my consciousness became one-pointed, forming a spearhead that eventually pierced through the veil to an inner path that seemed to be divine knowledge. Even the earliest glimpses or perceptions I was getting were great advances to the understanding and knowledge where my faith lies. A bridge was certainly built and traveled on.

However, as I advanced on the path, I was undergoing a significant change of direction that could be compared to a somersault. I became more concerned with inner realities of all of life, rather than their outward expression. As the emphasis shifted from my own external to internal aspects of my life, the deepening of my conscious being and awareness was accelerated.

I began seeing and sensing more than the physical and started to see that "different" side to people that many were not aware they had. I could see this in a gesture, such as a casual thank you, and I could sense it in eye contact, or even in the look of confusion when someone was searching for the right word. Some even became embarrassed when realizing their own holiness had been witnessed in a brief confrontation. I notice this often here in prison. *A Course in Miracles* explains this as "the blood of hatred fading to let the grass grow green again."

I became caught up with a deep awareness of myself and a deeper perception of the workings in the world. A refocusing of my consciousness occurred, which is now far-reaching. All of the avenues through which I conduct my search are radically transformed by my sincerity and the concentrated purpose of my efforts.

I no longer have to worry about my choice of words, like I once did when confronted with a subject I don't know the answer to. I simply respond, "At this point I cannot answer that." Anything I do comes from my heart with no exaggeration, unless, of course, it is a playful time with a little fun. I can honestly say that the depths of my internal understanding spread throughout my true essence, giving me new meaning and purpose in everything I do. I pursue my exploration with utmost exhilaration and with no exhaustion. I now find my seriousness to be fun.

It is Their purpose, meaning God, the Holy Spirit, and the Sonship, that sustains me. This is what is pictured as the face of Christ. I am getting the right amounts of sleep, food, and exercise. It seems effortless, but very much a *wanting*. I see a "different side" to my incarceration, and when I am released from prison will experience newer heights from this stepping stone. Because of Them which I am at one with, as are you, miracles have sprung up as do grass and flowers, on the once scorched and barren ground.

What my confusion has wrought, They have undone. The sinner and the saint that I once saw in me now appear to be waves on the surface of the same ocean, differing only in magnitude. Each are the natural outcome of forces in the universe rooted in time and causation, or, simply put, "cause and effect."

Although I have described the realization of divine knowledge as "traveling the path" to spiritual freedom, this analogy should not be taken literally. There is no ready-made road in the spiritual realm. Spiritual progress is not a matter of following an instruction manual to move along a line already laid down and unalterably defined. Rather, it is a creative process of spiritual involvement of the conscious mind. It is knowing why and when the ego wants to intrude. Rather than a path, this process is better described as a "spiritual journey."

The journey is comparable to a flight through the air, and not to a journey upon the Earth, because it is truly a pathless journey in literal terms. It is a dynamic movement within my consciousness that creates its own path and leaves no trace behind.

What is a hundred or a thousand years to Them or tens of thousands? Once They come to you and you accept Them you can begin your purpose. What never was—the illusion or the dream of separation, a fantasy world and life that you don't truly want—fades away and passes into nothingness when They come into your essence, and what is real is your own free will.

When you see yourself as fully absorbed with truth, you will see yourself as of the Sonship and constantly be seeing the face of Christ. The Sonship is in God Consciousness, where to know it is to exist as blissful power. To exist as a power is to know oneself as unbounded bliss; and to know oneself is to know Them. This is knowing divinity.

You are not living your free will in any existence in which power is limited, or knowledge imperfected, or joy clouded. This limited idea of who you are would make you a product of false imagination and cannot be the earnest seeker of spiritual freedom.

Chapter 28

Spiritual Freedom Now Realized

Spiritual freedom is obtained through God realization and is sometimes mistakenly considered to be the selfish aim of a limited individual for personal gain. But in reality there is no room for any such selfishness or limited realization. Rather, any gain—whether financial, to one's reputation, or otherwise—is the final aim of the limited and narrow life of the separated ego.

God realization is the result of the attainment of all the undoing of error the Sonship has accepted by the Holy Spirit. When you ask the Holy Spirit to undo some confusion you are having, you do this on behalf of the entire Sonship. Effects will be realized. This is so because truth is won through this undoing of errors we all make; and only then can God be realized. In this realization of truth you will gain expressions of a spontaneous and undivided life of love, peace, and harmony, because you have ruled out guilt. Material gain is not sought after; however, it often seems to flow into the life of those for whom it is the means necessary to fulfill their purpose. This is why you can never be lacking. The life of spiritual freedom is a pure blessing to all of humanity as it spreads. Don't be surprised if you have people say to you, "I want what you have."

What, then, remains to be undone for you to realize their presence? Many of us have different views of when attack is justified and when we think it is not to be allowed. But it's not unusual that when we perceive something as unfair, we think a response of anger is just. When we are angry at another, however, we are seeing what is the same as being different. The presence of any confusion over whether anger or attack is justified, in whatever form, will hide their presence, because they are not clearly known or not known at all.

Confused perception will block knowledge. It is not a question of the degree of confusion, or how much it interferes. Remember, the ego can play around with your perception, but cannot touch knowledge. Your confused perception shuts the door to Their knowledge and keeps what They know unknown to you.

What does it mean if you perceive attack in certain forms to be unfair to you? It means there must be some forms in which you think attack is fair. Otherwise, how could some instances be evaluated as unfair? Some, then, are given meaning and perceived as sensible, and some are seen as meaningless. So now, through the ego's tactics, this denies the fact that all are equally senseless, without cause or consequence, and cannot have effects of any kind. Their presence becomes obscured by this tainting to your perception by the ego, which stands between Their shining and your awareness that is your own, and equally belonging to every living thing along with you. Remember, God has no limits. What is limited cannot be Heaven; if you accept limitations as real, you must believe in a hell.

Unfairness and attack are one mistake, so firmly joined that where one is perceived, the other must be seen. You cannot be unfairly treated. The belief that you are is another form of the idea that you are being deprived by someone other than yourself. Projecting the cause of your sacrifice or sense of lack is at the root of everything you perceive to be unfair. But you are the one asking this of yourself and seeing the injustice. You have no enemy except to yourself, and make yourself enemy indeed to who you feel has unfairly treated you. Is it his or her fault that you don't know this divine brother/sister as you know yourself? But in the real world, aren't you the one being unjust? You have deprived this individual of what he is, denied him the right to be himself, and you are asking him to sacrifice for the ego in you.

Beware of the temptation to perceive yourself as unfairly treated. In this picture, you are seeking an innocence that is not Theirs (Father, Son, Holy Spirit) where as one is the divine YOU , but is yours alone only in illusion, at the cost of somebody else's guilt. Anytime the game of guilt is played, somebody must lose. Someone must lose innocence where someone else can take it from him, making it his own.

The Holy Spirit's purpose is to let the presence of your Holy Ghosts, including Him, be known to you. Nothing can be added to this purpose, as the world is purposeless except for this.

Therefore, simply ask the Holy Spirit to help you see Them as your invited Guests. God, the Holy Spirit, and the Sonship are as one. Just remember that you are of this party of Guests, which are the *knower*, the *known*, and *knowledge*. As you move into the spiritual realm at different moments and under different circumstances, ask yourself this question: Which one am I?

Chapter 29

Truth Will Correct All Errors

What else can correct illusions but truth? What are errors but illusions that remain unrecognized for what they are? Where truth has entered, errors disappear. They merely vanish, leaving not a trace by which to be remembered. They are gone because without belief they have no life. They disappear to nothingness, returning to whence they came. From dust to dust they go, but truth carries on.

Can you imagine what a state of mind it would be without illusion? How would it feel? The ego will tell you this is impossible.

Try to remember when there was a time, perhaps a minute, maybe even less, when nothing came to interrupt your peace. A period when you were certain you were loved and safe. Then, try to picture what it would be like to have that moment extended to the end of time and into eternity. Let the sense of quiet you felt be multiplied a hundred times and then a hundred more.

When truth has come, it wipes out illusion and there is no fear, no doubt, and no attack. When truth has come, all pain is over, because there's no room for transient thinking and for dead ideas to linger in your mind.

Truth cannot be found, but it can be won, and when it is, it is a permanent victory. It doesn't come to stay a while and change to something else. Illusions can never turn into truth.

Truth will correct all errors in your mind, which are telling you that you are separate from God. When you find yourself overwhelmed with confusion, understand that your mind is overloaded with errors. This was caused merely by the ego's tainting of your perceptions.

EXERCISE #4

Ask the Holy Spirit to undo the errors by using these words, or similar words of your own, in the form of a prayer. Keep it simple and use the type of language you would when talking to yourself. This is how I talk to the Holy Spirit within me:

Holy Spirit, my Teacher and Guide for life, I realize that truth will correct all errors in my mind. Please enforce truth within me so that I may see the real world in true light. I think I've let some crazy illusions take over. Thank you.

Each time you do this to correct errors in your mind, you are also speaking for the world, because along with Truth, you are one with it all.

PART V

KNOWING WHO YOU ARE

Chapter 30

Sharing Your Interpretations with Him

During the 1970s as a young man I was with the U.S. Air Force, and there was a conflict going on in the world involving the country of Angola. At that time I was stationed at an Air Force base in Texas, going through a survival training program. Basically, survival training is intense training to cope with the extreme, toughest of conditions imaginable, and to make life-sustaining decisions when you are for the most part alone and facing tremendous turmoil.

The squadron commander called us all together into a training classroom to inform our squadron that we were being flighted out that night to Angola, as ordered by President Ford. We were ordered not to make phone calls home or write letters for obvious security reasons. Needless to say, we were all stunned. We had not even finished our training program. At that point in our training we were learning about enemy tactics of propaganda, designed to promote in our minds perceptions of false and negative situations, causing an airman to make rash decisions.

That evening, with our full travel gear in check, we gathered at the designated meeting place, where Major Remming, our squadron commander, announced to us that we had been fooled. Although Angola was very much a conflict situation, the deployment orders were fake. They had fooled us in order that we might learn how our individual minds might react.

Earlier that day, before we realized the orders were phony and did actually believe we were going to a hostile area, Captain Jenkins, the psychologist who was our chaplain, gave us a talk about making split-second decisions. He urged us to carry along a message in our hearts. Then he described to us a dream he once had based on a common story.

"In this dream I was walking along the beach with my Lord," he told us. "Across the dark sky flashed scenes from my life. Each scene showed a time when I was not able to make decisions and was terribly confused. As I watched, I saw two sets of footprints in the sand, one belonging to me and one to my Lord.

"When the last scene of my life shot before me, I looked back at the footprints in the sand, and only one set of footprints remained. I realized that this was the lowest and toughest time of my life. This bothered me, and I questioned my Lord about my dilemma.

"'Lord, you told me when I decided to follow you that you would walk with me and talk with me, and help me along the way. But I see that during my hardest test, there is only one set of footprints. I don't understand why, when I needed you the most, you would leave me.'

"The Lord whispered to me: 'My child, I love you and will never leave you, for we are together. Where you saw only one set of footprints it was because I was carrying you.'"

Now, so many years later, I am often reminded of this story. *A Course in Miracles* teaches us that "Opposites must be brought together, not kept apart. For the separation is only in your mind."

Would you rather experience light or darkness? Knowledge and ignorance are both available for your choosing, but you can only have one or the other. Which do you truly want? When the two are brought together, whatever is not real will merely fade away, because only truth can unite. Ignorance cannot be truth, so all that remains at one with you is knowledge.

Perception is the "go-between" by which ignorance finds knowledge. But perception must be without deceit; otherwise, it becomes a messenger for ignorance to mock and deride while hoping to derail knowledge. True perception will carry ignorance into the open and welcoming arms of knowledge, where the search for truth ends and ignorance fades away joyfully.

The search for truth is an honest sorting out of everything that has gotten in your way and interfered with truth. This is where your errors come from, and this is why they can be so instantly undone by the Holy Spirit. By now I hope you accept the fact that truth simply is what it is. It speaks for itself; it cannot be lost and is always there. This is why it can't be found. Your seeking for it is not a search for truth, but a search for the means to accept what is already in you. Think about it.

You can hide from unwanted truth by covering it up with fear. But it is still there—just covered by illusion. Wherever you walk, you now walk in fear that you made, and the truth remains hidden. Then you feel guilt, because you know the truth is covered by your fear, thus generating more fear upon fear, and even fear of the pile of fears you made.

Have you ever tried to convince an unknowing individual about a matter that they truly do know but are hiding from? From their point of view, they tell you what you are saying is not true, because some important person said so. Yet it is true, and this "unknower" suspects that it is true, but will not admit it. Their inner suspicion is raised because God knows it to be true. All of their inner suspicion is really not a suspicion; it is a "knowing" that has been hidden away by fear.

Unknowing is therefore truly impossible. It was never a point of view or a certainty at all, but merely a belief in something that doesn't exist. Speaking truth to uncertainty does not make the uncertain thoughts more real. In fact, these uncertain thoughts will vanish once certainty stares them in the face.

The emphasis needs to be on bringing what is undesirable to you out in the open to face what is desirable. In other words, once you truly see what you do want, you will leave behind what you don't want—as in "never looking back." As we discussed earlier, what is past is now gone forever. By placing your thoughts on what you truly want, rather than on your past errors, you will automatically cast out illusions and "cause" fear to fade away.

You simply cannot have a belief in what you do not want, along with a belief in what you do want. These two systems of belief cannot coexist. It is really this simple: If you continually search after what you do not truly want, you will always get more of it. Now please bear with me here. If you will consciously bring out what you do not want and face it up against what you do want, your undesirables will instantly turn into nothingness. Anything that you truly do not want is not God's Will.

When your mind believes in total darkness, light cannot enter. Consider: When you close the blinds and shut the door to your home, the light will not enter until someone opens the door. Just sitting there in the dark and waiting will not let the light come shining through. This is what you are doing when you remain in an undesirable situation.

Truth does not struggle with ignorance, and love will not attack fear. You cannot defend yourself from fear. You can try, but all you will succeed at will be gaining more fear. God does not know of defense; therefore, truth does not need to be defended.

Defense is not of your own making, and the Holy Spirit will use your defenses on behalf of truth only because you made them. But with this method your defenses will see instantly that there is nothing to defend. Based on His purpose for you, He merely changes them into a call toward knowledge, which you will find not to be fearful at all.

Back in high school, when I anxiously and fearfully wanted to ask a lovely redheaded girl to the senior prom, I came up with all kinds of reasons why she would probably say no. But once I approached her and she said that she would love to go to the dance with me, I immediately found that the fear was gone.

When you ask the Holy Spirit to the dance, so to speak, He will always say yes.

As knowledge shows us there is nothing to fear, our knowledge increases at the same time our defenses dissipate. Therefore, ask the Holy Spirit, using your own words, to open the door and lift the blinds for the light to shine through. Share with Him your fears, by bringing all hidden secrets to the table. You must join and look at your fears along with Him. He will bring these fears and secrets to face the real and true you. Within an instant they will be undone.

Joining with Him in seeing is the way in which you learn to share with Him all of your interpretations that will lead you to knowledge. You cannot shift over to knowledge on your own. Sharing your true perceptions with Him, whom God has given you, teaches you how to recognize what you see.

Seeing with the Holy Spirit is not to be considered double vision, but merely the gentle fusing together of everything into one meaning, one emotion, and one purpose. Your Creator has one purpose, which He shares with you. This single vision that the Holy Spirit offers you will bring this oneness to your mind with clarity, and into your life for the world to accept.

Chapter 31

Sorting Out the False within You

Wouldn't you agree that the importance of learning is to accept the fact that you don't know? *A Course in Miracles* tells us: "Knowledge is power, and all power is of God."

Have you ever known an individual who seems to always have the answers to everything, including how to fix *your* problems? We all have run into this "know-it-all" somewhere along the line until, sooner or later, someone who knows better reveals the know-it-all's expertise to be not so expert, and he loses his power.

Everything we try to teach ourselves makes our own power more and more difficult to truly see. In many cases we end up finding that what we know is not the real knowledge we thought we had. We sense this as well. We may also end up making a show of strength that fails us. However, can we gain knowledge from what is false? What stands between us and the power of God is our learning of the false, and the ego's attempts to change truth into falsity.

Let all the false in you go, and be glad that you are no longer bound by it. This is how you can learn not to imprison yourself by trying to be something you are not. Can God learn to be something else? If you are of the Thought of God, then how can you be anything else? When you answer that truly, you are given all power by Him to be yourself, and you cannot learn to be powerless. Your power is in who you are. Is there anything you taught yourself that you truly prefer to keep, in place of what you really are? Is this the way you wish to live?

If you will live and learn by the Atonement—in other words, by being who you truly are—only then will you find your function that unites you with all of creation. You will know how to escape forever from what you taught yourself to this point in your life.

With this lesson, I now understand my friend Bill more truly, and why he rarely, if ever, introduces himself as a doctor. Bill is a foot doctor and has a successful podiatry clinic on the Gulf Coast of Florida. Often I have witnessed Bill, when asked by someone he just met what he does for work, respond something like: "I help people to feel more comfortable on their feet." Almost always they reply, "So, you must sell shoes, eh?"

Once, I invited Bill to play golf with my usual group of guys, with whom he was an unfamiliar but welcome guest. This time he explained further out of courtesy, saying that he ran foot clinics, where people of all ages with all kinds of foot problems would come, and he and his staff would do their best to treat and correct these ills. Naturally someone asked him if he was a doctor. Bill's reply was still quite humble: "Yes, some years ago I completed a doctoral degree in podiatry at Ohio State University." Then he simply left it at that, getting back to the golf match over a couple of bucks.

My good friend Bill does not define himself as a doctor of podiatry because it's not necessary for him to do so. Rather, he comes across as a person who enjoys helping others. Bill is what he is, a very joyful individual. His medical training as a podiatrist does not make him who or what he is. His schooling was something required of him in order to satisfy the worldly obligations expected of anyone who wishes to develop an expertise in fixing foot problems. This is all his degree means to him, and a foot doctor is not who Bill truly is.

All of your happiness lies in God's happiness for you, which is yours. But to accomplish this, you already know that you must bring all the dark lessons you taught yourself to the truth. You must face truth with your lessons, and you surely do know what these lessons are. This will prove to yourself that you no longer want the false, and will gladly exchange each falsehood for the bright lessons you were intended to receive. Your first lesson is already accomplished as you bring out your self-taught lessons for truth to see. This sets you on your way to spiritual freedom.

You might be asking yourself what these false lessons are or worrying that you don't know or cannot feel anything deep within. This is okay, because the fact that you do not know or feel confused tells you they are there. What's happening here is that you are still sorting out the untrue, and it may take some more sorting, which is fine. The process of undoing has started for you. But what you do not want to do is continue to add additional false lessons to the pile.

There is one test you can take with yourself, as sure as God, by which you will recognize if what you feel you are learning is true or not. If you are wholly free of fear of any kind, and if all of those who meet you, or even think of you, share in your perfect peace, you can then be sure that you have learned God's lesson and that nothing is promoted by the ego.

We all are going to have dark areas in our mind from time to time, as the ego continues to try and teach. But just as with Bill, where there are no dark areas he allows to hurt or hinder him, everyone around him sees his true light. Bill knows of the ego's presence and also knows that by his asking, the Holy Spirit will instantly step in to do some quick undoing.

The absence of peace in any of us means but one thing: You think that you do not have the same will that God wills for you. For every dark lesson the Holy Spirit replaces with a corrected one, and that you accept, you begin to see God's Will as your own free will. This is why Bill has a thriving medical practice with patients who adore him.

Don't be too concerned with how you can learn a lesson so completely different from everything that you taught yourself. How would you know? Your part is very simple. You only need to recognize that everything you learned was by teaching yourself what you really do not want. Simply ask the Holy Spirit to teach you, but do not use your experiences to confirm the false. This will only agitate you, keep you in the past, and keep peace away. When you are having unpeaceful times or feel disturbed in any manner, say to yourself:

> I don't know what any of this means and I don't know how to respond.

> I surely will not use my own past learning to guide me now.

By your refusal to attempt teaching yourself what you do not know, the Holy Spirit will step in and speak for you.

This is a miracle happening, and you cannot be your own guide to miracles, because it is you that made them necessary. Because you made the false, the means for undoing is the miracle being provided for you. The Holy Spirit will always be there through God whenever you need to turn to Him ever so little. It is impossible that He could ever get lost or lose His identity, because if He did, you would lose yours.

The miracle acknowledges His changelessness of the way He sees you as you always were. The miracle does not change you in order to fill an important slot or to keep up with current trends. It brings you back to who you truly were, and still are, before you started teaching and changing yourself. The miracle brings on the effects that the cause of guiltlessness started. In other words, your cause is being guilt free about who and what you are. The *effects* then will blossom.

After years of progressive hearing loss, by the age of forty-six the German composer and pianist Ludwig von Beethoven had become completely deaf. Nevertheless, he wrote his greatest music, including five symphonies, during his later years.

Was the miracle in Beethoven's abilities to play the piano, as well as compose? No, the miracle was within his acceptance of the God-given talents he had and that he recognized them to begin with. The miracle also continued in the fact that Beethoven lived his life pursuing and fulfilling the Will of God, which somehow Beethoven determined was also his own free will.

When he realized his hearing was gone, he could have easily perceived in himself that composing music was not his purpose and pursued something else. Instead, he went with his true gut feelings, regardless of his physical impairments. Had he not, his life may have been filled with guilt and regret. But the pure inner joy he did experience caused, in turn, more pure joy and peace to countless music lovers for all time to come.

Consider this with all your heart: "The Holy Spirit has freed you from the past and now He teaches you to accept His accomplishments as yours, and has made you free from what your ego made. All of His works are yours. He offers you a miracle with every undoing of your self-taught ways."

Chapter 32

You Are Entitled to Miracles

We are all of the Thought of God. Therefore, we are entitled to miracles, regardless of what we think or what the ego tells us. The ego doesn't understand miracles because this part of our "thinking" mind can only understand what is manmade. Anything that is manmade cannot be one with God. The truth within us is the One Thought of God, where His ideas come from, and which is what we are. The Holy Spirit is the communication aspect, and this is also who we are. Therefore, within this Oneness, which is our Divinity, He will undo the falsehood of our ego-based thoughts, causing miracles to take their intended path. Our journey to spiritual freedom is all in the undoing of all errors of the wrong-minded perceptions we taught ourselves.

Thus, our understanding of miracles can never lie in our illusions about ourselves. There are no magical powers we need to develop, nor any rituals to devise. It is inherent in the truth of what we are. It is guaranteed by the laws of God. We are entitled to miracles.

As an additional exercise, use this whenever a situation arises in which a miracle is called for to rid yourself of untruths.

EXERCISE #5

Close your eyes and remind yourself that you are asking for only what is rightfully yours. Be sure to first silence the ego, as it is not welcome here. You can do this by acknowledging its presence, as we discussed many times earlier on. The Holy Spirit will undo all that has been in the way and will grant your request.

Say to yourself with no ego involvement:

I am entitled to miracles. I will not trade miracles for self-taught ways of living.

As you do this exercise on a regular basis, whenever you feel as much as an inkling of false feelings or thoughts, you will be gaining control and power with your own thoughts. This in itself is a miracle.

Chapter 33

True Perception Begins the Miracle

There are certain opposites that simply do not attract. Light and darkness; everything and nothing—these cannot join together and coexist. Each one is either true or false. You either see light or you do not. Your thinking will become erratic until you can make a firm commitment to one or another. Which is it you want: Everything or nothing?

You cannot be fully committed to darkness, or nothing, because it is impossible. No individual has ever lived who has not experienced some light and "something." Therefore, how could anyone deny truth, totally? If you live in darkness, there is truth in that you are aware of light being available; it's just that you make efforts to block it. The same with nothingness: the truth is that the darkness you may live in is "something," in the fact that it is dark; therefore, it cannot be "nothing." Thus, no one can deny truth totally, though they may think they can, which is the illusion.

Have you ever thought of doing something, known it was wrong, but made the necessary excuses and proceeded to do it anyway? No one is ever partially innocent. Innocence is not partial, because it is real. Having innocent and true perception means that you never see what does not exist and will always see what does.

When you lack confidence in what someone will do, you are telling yourself that he is not of right-minded thinking. This cannot be a miracle-based way of seeing him, thereby denying the power of a miracle. You are not at one.

A miracle must perceive everything as it is. If only truth exists, right-minded thinking can only see perfection. It sees nothing else. Only what you create with the will of God has any real existence, which is innocent and truthful. The innocent cannot see from a distorted perception.

This was portrayed in the life of Thomas Edison, the greatest inventor in American history. When he first attended school in Port Huron, Michigan, his teacher complained that he was "too slow" and hard to handle. As a result, Edison's mother decided to take her son out of school and teach him at home. His own mother, now teaching him, discovered her son was fascinated with science, and when he was ten years old, she set him up with a chemistry laboratory. Eventually he produced in his lifetime more than 1,300 inventions.

When Thomas Edison invented the lightbulb, he tried over 2,000 experiments before he got it to work. A young reporter asked him how it felt to fail so many times. He said, "You don't understand; I never failed once. Inventing the lightbulb happened to be a 2,000-step process."

A mind can miscreate only when it believes it is not free; and this is probably why Thomas Edison was uncomfortable in school. Of course, school in those days was much different. Nevertheless, his mother sensed his imprisoned mind, which was holding her son back. His mind was limited and not free to assert itself. To be one is to be of God's Will, as well as one mind. When the will of Thomas Edison and the Thought that created him were at one, this perfect accord was the making of a miracle.

Nothing could prevail against Edison when he commanded his spirit into the hands of his Source. All sense of separation disappeared, and he awakened to the call of his purpose. Was the invention of the lightbulb his purpose? Additionally, was it a miracle? "No" is the answer to both. It was how he lived his life that was his purpose, and the process itself was the miracle, which resulted in the world having the light literally turned on.

Each of the 2,000 steps was the Divine guidance he was receiving. He was being taught what did not work, and to leave in what did. He was being shown how to shut the door on "nothingness" and open the door for "everything," each step of the way, until he helped the light shine forth.

This single purpose of the Holy Spirit allowed the cause of perfect imagination, not only in Edison, but to countless individuals who were able to tap into it. This imagination establishes the presence of God. Yet the vision can be perceived only by the truly innocent. Could we say the same for Edison's mother, who had the inspiration to take her son away from the schoolhouse?

A Course in Miracles teaches us: "When truth is realized, the hearts that are pure and innocent defend true perception instead of defending themselves against it." By understanding the lesson of the Atonement, or At-one-ment, you are without a wish to attack; you allow yourself to see truly and will not miscreate. This is what the Bible really means when it says, "When He shall appear (or be perceived) we shall be like Him, for we shall see Him as He is."

When you have distorted views, you need to correct them—to withdraw your faith in them by investing it only in what is true. How simple can this be? No one can make an untruth become true. If you are willing to accept what is true in everything you perceive, you will let it be true for you. Truth overcomes all errors, and those who live in error and emptiness can never find lasting peace.

If you can perceive truly that you are canceling misperceptions in yourself and in others, you will be seeing yourself, as well as others, for what they truly are. By doing this you are letting them know that you see the truth in them, regardless of any brave front that smiles fictitiously. Your acceptance of their truth allows them to accept it for themselves, and make the decision to heal, and to cross over the bridge with you to right-mindedness—thereby inducing a miracle.

Chapter 34

The Bridge to Knowledge

You are seeing the bridge over to right-minded perception, and now you are ready to see the bridge from there, over to knowledge. The travel over this bridge cannot be forced; it just simply flows or happens. No one forces themselves to know.

Do you truly know God as a beneficent order to all things? By now you should be sensing Him as the Thought that causes everything to happen without human conscious control. This "knowing" will allow you to realize the depth of your own abilities, thereby bringing out your real strength. Can you see in your daily life the working of this One Thought? Do you feel as though you can relax and know that you have a function that will be carried out?

Much of the world's people question and doubt their function, thereby accepting illusion, only because they are afraid of their true potential. If we live our life this way, we become incapable of knowledge because we perceive only for personal gain and not for love. We are never able to leave the bridge of perception. The separated mind brings on varying degrees, aspects, and intervals, making perception the measuring device for remaining separated. Such as: "How much must I sacrifice to achieve that goal?"

Our physical body does get involved with our perceptions, often causing stress. The body is at work every moment and does respond to these stresses and even to the joys we experience. We do understand and are in awe of the fact that our body is a brilliance of design, an array of mechanisms and efficiency our human efforts have never begun to match. Our heart expands and contracts, pumping blood to microscopic cells that feed us, make our hair grow, and do all that makes us a living being.

Planets revolve around the sun, seeds become flowers, embryos become babies, and all with no help from us. All this movement is built into a natural system, and you and I are each an integral part of that system. We can let our lives be directed by the same Thought, or we can do it ourselves as humankind has tried to do ever since the separation—what some call the symbolic "Tree of Knowledge," where the first bite of illusion was digested.

When the separation first occurred, a level of perception called consciousness became a part of our mind. A "separate" part, if you will. This level of the conscious mind made itself a perceiver, rather than a creator. This is where the ego built its domain, and we have been perceiving ever since. As we discussed earlier in this book, our minds are no longer whole, now occupied by the ego, which is a wrong-minded attempt to perceive yourself as you wish. The ego helps you to make it difficult to know who you truly are.

The ego is full of questions, including how it was made, rather than how it was created. The ego is good at asking questions but not at receiving meaningful answers, because any answers would involve knowledge that cannot be perceived by the ego. With this, the mind becomes confused, because only One-Mindedness can be without confusion. How can a divided and separated mind not be confused? It is uncertain about what it is. Being that it is out of accord with itself, it must be in conflict. This makes all separated parts strangers to each other, and this is the essence of defense, where attack is prepared. No wonder we are afraid of our real potential.

With the habitual dominance of the ego, you have become fearful of yourself and may be finding it hard to escape from who you made yourself to be. But you can, right now, at this very moment, easily escape from your misperceptions because they are not true. These misperceptions of yourself are errors; but your creation is beyond error, and with the truth that you are, your split-mind can be healed.

Let's not confuse right-mindedness with knowledge. Your right-mind is only applicable to right-minded perception, which does lead to knowledge. Right-mindedness when properly utilized is the correction for wrong-mindedness, and is the state of mind that gives you accurate perception rather than confusion. There will be some doubt, but that's okay, because anything not of knowledge will surely have its doubts. We can call this *miracle-minded perception*, because miracles can only be possible by the corrected perception that begins the healing process.

If your perception is confused over any matter, big or small, bring it to the Holy Spirit for accurate perception. Your confused perception will be transcended to a clear outlook of the matter, preparing the groundwork for a shift over to knowledge. Traveling the bridge over to knowledge need not be a long journey; quite often it is instantaneous. Regardless of the time it takes to arrive at knowledge, He will have you perceiving in a positive and fresh way—just as how, with my incarceration, I am seeing positive avenues leading me out of prison and into a new and rewarding life. Of course I see a lot of negative experiences each day; but I am seeing the negative as fuel for the road ahead. This is what I mean by right-minded perception. It's *how* you look at it.

Perception in general always involves some misuse of your mind because it brings your mind into areas of uncertainty. Otherwise, it wouldn't be perception. The mind is very active, and when it chooses to be separated it can only perceive. But it does desire to know, and chooses carefully out of uncertainty when it perceives.

Even when we think about the process of our mind, we see it in a physical sense, often relating it to our brain, rather than our connection to the universe. As well, the universe I talk about here does not entail the stars, moon, and the galaxies we gaze at on a beautiful night. The universe I speak of here is literally meant to mean "all that is real."

Of course, externally, the physical universe we can see does support our physical existence. Photosynthesis in plants and plankton in the ocean produce oxygen that we need in order to breathe. It is important to respect the laws that rule the physical universe, because violation of these laws threatens our survival. When we pollute the oceans or destroy plant life, we are destroying our support system, and thus are destroying ourselves.

Internally—meaning within our true essence, that inner altar where we abide—is the universe that supports our survival as well, both emotionally and psychologically. The internal equivalent to oxygen is love, which comes from our spirit. What really is our spirit? you are probably wondering. It's quite simple. It is the total, undeniable truth that you are. This is not perceived by us, but it is known.

If we are perceiving out of greed we cannot find truth. The function of perception is to interpret. This permits you to misinterpret your body as who you truly are, in an attempt to escape from the conflict you made. Knowledge does not do anything, especially not interpret, because it already knows. However, other ego minds might perceive knowledge as an attacker, though it cannot attack. What these egos might perceive as an attack from knowledge is that knowledge cannot lose, but the attacker is really perception in conflict.

Your mind will return to its proper function, leaving behind all your subordinate functions the ego made, only when *it wills to know*. Then it becomes in the service of spirit, where perception is changed. This will produce gradual overriding of perception by knowledge, when truth is tapped into. When truth and knowledge are one, you will know this as spirit. The part of your mind that will hang onto perception cannot separate itself from spirit, and will be joyfully bridged over to knowledge. Spirit is where the power to create abides, and the more it creates, the more right-minded perception will cross the bridge to knowledge. Knowledge will increase. Perception needs translation and transcending, but knowledge does not.

Therefore, the laws of the universe merely describe the way things truly are. The laws were not invented by man. They are discovered. They are not dependent on our body or spirit. Spirit is merely one with these laws.

All things made by the separation are in conflict, because they are meaningless to each other. Their only function is for themselves. Spirit has no conflicting degrees that are either measured or translated. God the Father, the Sonship, and the Holy Spirit are each a level within the Trinity, and are the only levels capable of Unity. Spirit is union, and you as spirit are of the Trinity.

Chapter 35

Knowing Your Spirit—That Knows God

You've probably heard it said before: "The abilities each of us possesses are only shadows of our real strength." This in itself is a perception that is inherently judgmental and that is introduced by separated minds.

What we perceive as our physical structure called the body, which is subject to disease, old age, death, and dust, is not ultimately you. It is a misperception of your essential reality that is beyond birth and death. This misperception is due to the limitations of what we perceive. Most of what we believe comes from what we perceive, and unfortunately this perception leads to illusory faith—a faith built on perceptions outside ourselves. But even with this illusory faith, we do know deep within that something is not exactly right. We can sense it. Nevertheless, many continue to go with the ways that were laid out for them, so focused on our physical existence that we lose touch with the essence of our true being—the essence that gave us the "not exactly right" feeling. Our attraction to the physical justifies our states of fear.

Don't turn yourself away from the body, however, because within this temporary structure is the splendor of your essential and immortal reality. What do I mean by "within" your body? It is the space between the cells and atoms, veins, arteries, and corpuscles. All of the space within you is your inner body, and this is where the eternal you exists.

For your time here on Earth, you can liken all physical structure of your body to a fence around, or surrounding, all that is real. It is the space between the heart muscles that makes them contract. Just as with music, it is the space between the notes that gives the symphony its life. Likewise, don't turn your attention elsewhere in your search for Truth, because it is nowhere to be found but within.

Since the separation, the words "create" and "make" have become confused with each other. When you make something, you do so out of a specific lack or need. Anything "made" for a specific purpose is to enhance something physical. When you make something to fill a perceived lack, you are implying that you believe in separation. The ego has made many ingenious thought systems for this purpose. Not one of them is creative. It's all wasted effort to gain more. No matter how much stronger or more beautiful you make the fence, it will not enhance the space between. The energy that is your power, and which is created by thought, is the beauty that emanates from the space within.

Don't fight against the body, because in doing so you are only fighting against your own reality. At this time in eternity, which is the only time eternity has, your invisible inner body is housed within this structure that you call you. This is who you are. Through your inner body you are inseparably connected to That One Life, which is birthless, deathless, and eternally present. This is where your knowledge is and where you know God.

Knowing does not lead to doing. The confusion you have between your real creation, or inner self, and what you made of yourself from perceptions is so vastly profound that it becomes impossible for your body to know anything. Knowledge is always stable and quite evident. But you as your body are not. Nevertheless, you are perfectly stable as God created you. In this sense, when your behavior is unstable you are disagreeing with God's Idea of your creation. You can do this if you choose, but you would hardly want to do it if you were in your right mind, using right-minded perception.

The fundamental question we all continually ask ourselves cannot properly be directed to ourselves at all. We keep asking ourselves, "What is it we are?" This implies that the answer is not only one you don't know, but is also one that is up to you to supply. Yet you cannot perceive yourself correctly. You have no image to be perceived. The word "image" is always perception related and not a part of knowledge. Images are symbolic and stand for something else. The idea of "changing your image" recognizes the power of perception, but also implies that there is nothing stable to know.

Knowing is not open to interpretation, and it is experienced only when you are in a state of permanent connectedness with your inner body; feeling it at all times. This will rapidly deepen and transform your life. You may try to interpret this knowledge, but this will only bring you back to perception. This occurs when we regard ourselves as separated and unseparated at the same time—which, of course, is impossible. This is when you need to let go of all separated thoughts. By your asking, the Holy Spirit will gladly undo these separated thoughts.

Consider this: The key for you now is to bring your inner conscious thoughts directly into your inner body—that space between the "notes" that make your "music." You will build up a vibrational frequency the source of which is your real thought— your pure thought that is not of illusion. The frequency will become much like a light that is connected to a dimmer switch. As you increase the energy level, all wrong-minded perception will leave your consciousness, and only right-mindedness will be available. The light increases as the dimmer switch releases energy (pure thought) and shines on the bridge to knowledge. You will see new circumstances welcoming your crossing. Now you will "know" what to do.

As long as you are in conscious connectedness with your inner body, you are like a tree that is deeply rooted in the earth or a building with a deep foundation. This analogy was used by Jesus when he walked this earth, in the misunderstood parable about the two men who build their houses. One man builds on sand without a foundation, and where storms and floods come sweep the house away. The other man digs deep until he reaches rock.

This man's house does not get swept away by disasters. Deep within us, inside the space that makes the music, is the foundation that Jesus wanted us to realize, and not perceived external belief systems made by man.

Prayer is a way of asking for something. But the only meaningful prayer is for forgiveness, because those who have been forgiven have everything. Once forgiveness has been accepted, prayer in the real sense becomes utterly meaningless. The prayer for forgiveness is nothing more than a request that you may be able to recognize what you already have—for example, the space between the notes that "creates" your symphony.

Don't give all of your attention away to the inner body. By all means, focus on what you are doing, but feel the inner body at the same time, as though it is background music, whenever and wherever possible. Stay rooted within. Then observe how this changes the quality of your initial perceptions on a new undertaking. See how often you are of right-minded thinking, and most of all, how often you just seem to "know."

When challenges occur, go within and make it a habit to focus as much as you can on the inner energy (pure thought) field within you. This is what right-mindedness breathes as its oxygen. Knowledge is merely the result. Any response you will need for any given situation will come from this energy. This is how God works in "mysterious ways."

Truth can only be known. All of it is equally true, and knowing any part of it is to know all of it. Only perception involves partial awareness. Knowledge is all one and has no separate parts. When you are one with it, then you will know yourself. This knowing is spirit, and spirit knows God.

Chapter 36

Let Your Breath Take You to That Place Within

I began learning the game of golf as a teenager and continued through my adult life. One thing about golf is that it does grab your spirit. There are times while playing a round of golf when, even if just for a moment or two, you leave all distractions behind while focusing on the execution of a particular shot. Then, once the job is complete, good or bad, you return your attention and state of mind to the camaraderie of your playing companions. An avid, serious golfer will often spend countless hours on the driving range, grinding away at a particular aspect of his or her game. Often this can be considered or compared to "going within."

A story is told of the late, world-renowned golf champion Ben Hogan, who was playing in a Ryder Cup match in the 1950s. In those days, the Ryder Cup was a team event between the United States and Britain. Hogan, an American player, was on the driving range before a match, fine-tuning his golf swing, and was known by all the other golfers as loving to "grind" ball after ball on the range. He was pounding his driver out there, about 230 yards on the fly with a slight left-to-right direction of his ball flight, called a "fade." His caddy was standing out there with a baseball mitt, catching each shot and placing the balls on a stack. His caddy did not have to move, due to the accuracy and precision of each shot Hogan made. One right after another, as spectators were amazed.

A member of the British team happened to be watching Hogan practice and said to him, "I say, Ben, I believe I could help you with a bit of advice to correct that fade of yours." Hogan did not reply, nor did he acknowledge the golfer's presence. It was as though Hogan didn't know he was there.

The Brit blurted out again, "I say, Ben—oh Ben, did you hear me? I say, Ben, if you'd drop your right hand a bit under the grip you'd be able to cure that fade."

Hogan continued to pound ball after ball like a machine, directly into his caddy's baseball mitt, as a good-sized pile of balls grew at his side. In the middle of Hogan's golf swing, he softly spoke to the British player: "Why do I need a cure? You don't see my caddy moving, do you?"

I have discovered that the best way for me to go deep within is through my breath. I do this in the form of meditation, when I have some quiet and private time alone. The key is to use your breath and try to feel the energy of your inner body as you relax.

You will want to feel the expanding and contracting of your abdomen along with your breath, as an energy field. Go within and feel it. Even if you are standing in line or stuck in a traffic jam, any outside noise can simply be heard as background static outside of your energy field, just as Hogan sensed the interference of the British golfer as nothing more than backstage sounds. The energy you feel is the truth in you. Try to be a part of it, and relax while you feel your breath entering and occupying all space within you—within that "fence" that surrounds who you are.

The most efficient way for me to practice this is to lie flat on my back on a comfortable surface. I find it easy to visualize; therefore, in this meditation I see myself surrounded by a glorious light. I will see myself in a swimming pool under the water, but rather than water, I am submerged in a luminous substance that is breathable. I breathe in this luminous, glowing light, feeling it fill up all space that exists within my body, thereby becoming that glow. Then I will focus on myself being the light that is able to shine darkness away. Additionally, with every out-breath, I see the glow radiate out of me and into the world. Any luminous glow that leaves me is replaced on my next in-breath.

Whenever I need a solution to a problem, or feel a sense of fear over a given matter, or if I am in need of a creative idea, I stop my thinking and bring my attention to my luminous energy field. I feel the stillness of the light. Rather than thinking with my brain, I'll "illuminate" my inner body. God is the energy field of my inner body.

At different times throughout your day, remind yourself that you are able to hear God's Voice without interrupting your regular activities in any way. The part of your mind in which Truth abides is in constant contact or communication with the whole Sonship, whether you are aware of it or not. This is the extension of God. The other part of your mind functions in the world and obeys the world's laws. It is this part that is constantly distracted, disorganized, and highly uncertain.

The part of you that is listening to the Voice *for* God is calm, always at rest, and wholly certain. The Voice for God, which is the Holy Spirit in you, is really the only part of your mind there truly is. Any other part is a wild illusion that is not real. Try to always remember this as you listen to it. Always try to identify with the part of your mind that is calm, cool, and collected. This is where the Holy Spirit is relaying God's Will to you. Always here, and no other part of your mind.

On a regular basis throughout your day, whether for a lengthy period or a brief break in your activities, try to actually hear God's collected coolness in your mind. This is His Voice through the Holy Spirit who is reminding you of Him, and of yourself as one Thought. Believe it or not, these calm, collected, and cooling thoughts are your holiness at work. Holiness does not require special candles or incense, or oils, waters, beads, or clothing. It only requires confidence and knowing that you are joining your will with the Will of God; in other words, your acceptance of His Will as yours. The Holy Spirit, through cause and effect, helps you to make this happen. These are the holiest and happiest thoughts you can have.

If any frantic or erratic thoughts start to surface, that's okay. Simply acknowledge their presence as illusion, say hello, then gently but firmly say good-bye, shut the door on them, and proceed back to your breathing.

Listen in deep silence. Feel your heart pump blood through your veins, and open up your mind. Go past all the illusory imaginings that cover your real thoughts and past the sights and sounds of this insane world controlled by ego. It is okay to notice background distractions, such as a loud car engine or an irate person nearby. Tell yourself that you do not live there. You are trying to reach your real Home. You are trying to reach the place where you are truly welcome. You are reaching God, and He welcomes you.

Repeat these words periodically in your day, with your eyes open or closed: *"God's Voice speaks to me all through the day."*

If you're at home and sitting in a comfortable chair, you may want to close your eyes and take some time with this. Or if you are standing in line, say at the bank or post office, as you contend with the world around you, realize you are consciously inviting God's Voice to come through your mind and into you.

Do this as often as necessary, making it a habit, getting good at it, and bringing yourself Home. Now you are seeing that *"There is another way of looking at the world."*

Chapter 37

Accepting Atonement for Yourself

Going within is where you will accept Atonement. It's where you will witness it happening. How is it that you accept Atonement? It happens when you come to a decision to accept yourself as God created you. It's the chosen direction you take that is real. But what really is a choice? It can only reflect some uncertainty as to what you are. Where there is no choice, there is no doubt that can deeply root itself. As you practice asking for Guidance and hearing the Voice for God, you will have no questions about your oneness because there is no thought, other than the One Thought that sustains you. With this, there can be no conflict in the question: "What or who am I?" In this alone you've discovered freedom.

"What or who am I?" How could you even be able to ask yourself this question, except for the fact that you don't recognize yourself? Refusing to accept yourself as you are could make this question bothersome to you. The only thing that is surely known by any living thing is that it is what it is. You see other individuals, and certainly animals, as who they are, but you struggle with yourself. Why the uncertainty?

Consider this: "Your own uncertainty about what you must be is self-deception on a scale so vast, its magnitude can hardly be conceived," says *A Course in Miracles*.

Living your life and not knowing yourself is equal to believing that who you *truly* are—the One Thought of God—does not exist. Often we have an insight into who we are or what our true purpose might be, but we are quick to put it off as fantasy: "I'm not meant to be an author of a popular book" or "I must be crazy to think that I could ever become a doctor." This type of thinking makes the ego feel satisfied and secure. However, real joy will not come about. Isn't life about being yourself?

Deep inside, we all know the truth of who we are. So what are we doing when we ask, "Who am I?" We are suggesting that we are not ourselves, and therefore have chosen to be something else. It is this "something else" that becomes the questioner of what that "something" is. But how could we be alive without knowing the answer? Still, we may *think* we do not know. The separated ego judges against our true being and denies its worth, so we decide that we do not know the only certainty by which we have been living.

As we continue to become uncertain of our life, we deny what is truly meant to be. Because of this denial we need Atonement. This denial makes no change in what we are, but we have split our mind into what knows and what does not know the truth. You are yourself; there is no doubt of this. Yet you still ask "Who am I?" You do not ask what part of your split-mind can really doubt yourself. In reality, there can be no part of the real you that asks this question. The real you knows, and to know means there is no question. The question simply does not arise.

Atonement is your acceptance that anything of the separation is not real. What is unreal is not of God. It is nothing. Your acceptance of this remedies the strange idea that it is possible to doubt yourself and be unsure of what you really are. This is madness. Yet, it is the universal question of the world. What does this mean, other than that the world is mad? Why would we share this madness in the sad belief that what is universal, in this sense, is true?

Nothing the world believes is true. It is a place whose purpose is to be the home where those who claim they do not know themselves can come to question what it is they are. This will continue with all who arrive into this world until the time Atonement is accepted. This will be when all can learn it is impossible to doubt and not to be aware of what we are.

Your acceptance of this reality is only asked for from the part of you that is certain. Our oneness is set forever in the Mind of God, and in your own. We all have a mission here. We cannot continue, for generations to come, to reinforce the madness humanity believes in. Let's not forget the goal we are accepting. It is more than just our own happiness we come to gain. What we accept as what we are, proclaims what everyone must be along with us. Don't fail your brothers, or you fail yourself. Look lovingly on them, that they may know that they are part of you, and you of them. Don't be too quick to assume that they don't know.

This is what we learn from Atonement, and it demonstrates that the oneness of God's Son is unassailed by any question that we do not know what we are. Therefore, right now at this very moment, you can accept Atonement, not to change reality, but merely to accept the truth about yourself and go your way rejoicing in the endless Love of God. It is this that we are asked to do.

Accepting Atonement within yourself takes only an instant. Simply tell your Guide that you want to Atone—to be At-One—and it will be done. To keep this reinforced in you, periodically throughout your day, every day, say or think these words:

> I have accepted Atonement for myself, and I remain as
> God created me.

We have not lost the knowledge that God gave to us when He created us like Him; He extended His Thought as the Idea He created. We can remember it for those who have not yet been able to accept Atonement for themselves, because creation in all our minds is as one. Allow your mind to be cleared of all the illusory cobwebs, and learn to keep the knowledge of yourself as a part of your awareness, without needing a choice.

PART VI

THE ANSWER TO ALL THAT IMPRISONS YOU

Chapter 38

The Ego's Lessons for Imprisonment

Leave it to the ego to always have you questioning something, especially when the truth is plain to see. Who would know what your true reality is? The ego thinks it does, but is uncertain. All day long the ego tries to teach us how we should act, what to say, and who or what not to say it to. But the ego doesn't understand anything that is real, because it views the world with wrong-minded perceptions that it invented or, we can say, "dreamed up." Therefore, what kind of a teacher can it be? So why do we always follow its lessons? The answer to both these questions is simple. We tell ourselves the ego is the best teacher ever because of "what a wise man once said." Or, "They've been doing it this way for generations, so there must be some trick to it." Or, "You will be forever damned in hell if you try to change now." Does any of this sound even a little bit familiar?

Any of the ego's lessons we try to learn are always of fear. But it is your choice to accept lessons of either love or fear, truth or falsehood, reality or unreality. There is no middle ground. Now that you are realizing "There is a different way of looking at the world," you can easily make your decision. Even if you could disregard the Holy Spirit's lessons of truth completely, which is impossible, you would still learn nothing from the ego because the ego is nothing. How can something you made up teach you anything? It's ridiculous, right? But could this possibly be the reason that history repeats itself? The ego loves history because it is sold on the past, and it is selling it to you.

Why would anyone choose a teacher like this? Doesn't the total disregard of anything it teaches make sense? Do we wish to keep passing these lessons along? We must, because there sure are more powerful bombs and other killing devices today, at my age of fifty-five, than there were when my grandfather was my age. Why do we continue to pass these lessons along?

Is this the teacher that our all-loving Creator would appoint to help us find ourselves? Clearly the answer is no, and this is why we are so filled with guilt. Do you still insist on following the demands of the ego? If its demands are not enough, the ego has done more harm to our learning, and our healing, than any of the unhappiness it additionally has given us. Wouldn't you agree that learning should be joyful if it leads you along your natural path and facilitates the development of what you have within you? "The learning of what?" you are likely asking.

I'm sure you'll agree that everything we face in life is a learning experience, including the illnesses we talked about earlier that can seem to attack our bodies. We're taught against our true nature, and this imprisons us. An example might be the prayers dished out as a punishment when we feel a child needs to learn a lesson, where we believe penance is appropriate. Why would we teach a child to associate prayer with punishment? Nevertheless, we are taught, and we teach, to sacrifice. But your own true free will is of your nature; therefore, you cannot go against it. If you truly can sense, or have the knowledge of, your free will, then the ego's lessons will not sink in. This adds to the light that draws the ego's lessons to it, where they fade away in plain sight—the plain sight that is your *real vision*.

It is not in our free will to be imprisoned, and of course I can literally vouch for that. Our true free will is all about freedom. This is why the ego is against free will and why the ego believes freedom requires sacrifice and hard work. The Holy Spirit's lesson to us is that our will and God's Will cannot be out of accord, because they are one. How could it be possible that the Holy Spirit, which is the Spirit of God, and God Himself, be separate? Therefore, if you are of God, how can you be separate too? How simple can this be?

The ego tries to teach us that as a sinner we have a desire to oppose God's Will and makes us think that God's Will is for the weak or for those who have trouble in life. What is it we are usually thinking about, or what occurrences seem to come about when we hear someone say, "It must be God's Will, so let it be done?" But when someone writes a book and it sells millions of copies around the globe, and is translated into many different languages, and the result is that it touches and changes many lives for the good, what is said then? Do we hear comments that suggest this must be the work of the Holy Spirit? Usually not, but sometimes, yes. Most often people will be skeptical or critical, and this has been the case with *A Course in Miracles*. The comments range from "This is unbelievable" to a whole line of armchair negative critics who focus only on the amount of money from sales of the book. The *Course* is distributed by the not-for-profit organization called The Foundation for Inner Peace. And guess what? The Holy Spirit has the thought system that knows that the negative critics are necessary, so the material—three books or the condensed version—gets the exposure needed.

The late Helen Schucman, a Columbia University professor and an atheist who was conservative in theory, in 1965 at age fifty-six, received an instructional voice, beginning a ten-year process of transcribing the 1,200-page spiritual teaching called *A Course in Miracles*. She only took credit for transcribing the words and never claimed authorship—but she did declare the voice to belong to Jesus. The core message is forgiveness and has helped millions of people worldwide to release fear and find greater love in their lives—and still remains a mystery to many.

The *Course*, as it is often called, does not aim to replace the Bible, nor is it a cult, for that would require an idol. For myself and countless others, the *Course* has opened my mind to a point that I now have clear, ego-free understanding of both Old and New Testament writings. I get more from scripture now. Involving oneself with the *Course* as I have gives one an indispensable personal companion that takes one on a powerful yet often misunderstood spiritual path.

Are you now seeing why we are so often afraid of the truth? Think about it. When you decide not to go along with the crowd on a particular issue or a decision needing to be made, because something burning inside you is telling you this is not God's Will, doesn't it initially make you feel a bit uncomfortable, or maybe even a little fearful? You might be firm on your stance, but there is also room for anxiety, at best. This is the ego in you having a temper tantrum and not coping with your revolt very well. It is also concerned about what the other egos might think. It is concerned because egos don't truly know one another and are frightened about what to expect. Friends end up no longer as friends.

You must begin considering that the lessons of the ego cannot be learned, and any attempt to learn them is a violation of your own freedom. This can make you feel more afraid of your own true free will, because of the fact that it is truly free. Please look hard at this. To the ego, what is free must be fought for and sacrificed for in some fashion. This usually involves some kind of attack. Therefore, any attempt to learn it is fighting for it.

In America, we take pride that we have fought for our freedom. But what do we do once we have it? In her book *The Shelter of Each Other*, Mary Pipher, Ph.D., found that in countries where citizens can get killed for voting, they maintain an inner freedom that results in a voter turnout higher than in America, where it's safe and easy.

The Holy Spirit opposes any imprisoning of the will of a Son of God, knowing that your free will is also God's Will. The Holy Spirit's method for your learning is in a natural way. There is no "attempting" necessary. This is why much earlier on in this book we discussed the types of freedom usually sought after by humanity. Your Guide, your true loving gut feeling, takes you along the road to freedom, directing you how to look beyond or how to disregard anything that holds you back.

This "looking beyond" and "disregarding" is where forgiveness plays its part. This is often needed by you when grief plays a part as friends or family members turn their backs on you for what you may have once done, or have not done, based on how they view a certain situation that has caused upset. Rather than remaining stuck in a mold of ill feelings and a poor attitude, you can choose to look beyond by overlooking whatever it was in their own mind that led them to their decision to reject you. You cannot allow a mindset of another to hold you back. By letting go with forgiveness, you can move on with no further discomfort toward them. This allows you to choose to change your own mindset by releasing it to the Holy Spirit. But you must be operating from *Truth*.

Chapter 39

The Holy Spirit's Lessons for Freedom

The Holy Spirit teaches us the difference between imprisoning our mind or being free. But have you ever at times told yourself you were free, when deep within you could feel the chains binding you to something? Your ego may be mumbling inside your brain right now, wondering what the hell am I talking about. But you also may have a voice in your heart saying, "Yeah, I know what he means here."

The truth is we do imprison ourselves. Consider how the world teaches us the meaning of "hard work." We like to apply the word "work" to the things we think the world rewards us for, making us feel accepted. After all, isn't this what "happy hour" was designed for? How about a "hard day's work" or "a long week at work?" Or, even more exciting, "working at your marriage" and even "working on your relationship with God." Is "work" really what is required? We imprison ourselves with "work" in order to gain freedom, money, love, and faith. But wait, there's more. Doesn't the ego teach us that we must sacrifice "this" in order to get "that?"

Most of my adult life I have had a passion for the game of golf. I have met many wonderful people and formed terrific friendships due to my participation in this godsend of a sport. These individuals know who they are, and I send my greetings to them through this book.

With golf, the object is to smack the little ball around the course and into a small hole, using the least amount of smacking (strokes) as possible. The lowest score is a winner. Anyone who understands the game of golf realizes it can be frustrating at times. It has been perceived by golfers gradually over time, since golf began in the 1800s, that in order to lower your average score, called a handicap, you should "work" on your game. This should entail consistent practice and ongoing lessons from a golf professional. Practicing every aspect of one's game is often considered to be a "never-ending job." I always worked hard on my game, which often put stress on my expectations when I would go out to "play." In other words, there was a time when I was much too serious. I would try to force an outcome. That was until my good ole friend Ron talked some sense into me.

Ron always seemed to enjoy golf for the game it was meant to be, regardless of his score, and he could care less about any such practice. He would often see me at the driving range, which can be fun in itself. But with me it was a constant grinding on my golf swing to shave a few strokes from my handicap. One day Ron said to me, "Jimbo, why do you work so hard at playing a game?" He earnestly talked to me, over time, about just "playing" the game and letting go of the work. His words gradually sent me out to play without worrying so much about my outcome. Need I say that my scores and handicap improved naturally and that I was having fun without the work? That was by far the best golf lesson I ever had.

Another friend, and low handicapper as well, Dirty Mike, always said, "Let's all go out today and shoot lights out, by having fun." (You are probably wondering how Dirty Mike got his name. All I can tell you is that it has something to do with being "dirty" in a playful manner. I promised him years ago I would keep the secret. It is his secret and is part of what keeps him a fun-loving friend.) Like me, Dirty Mike was no angel either when it came to giving up his soul to the competition; he and I were always at each other's throat in grudge matches. But Mike was able to take the competition to a level that still kept it enjoyable for him. Dirty Mike was quick to turn around any wrong-minded thoughts that led him away from the pure joy of the competition, by shifting them into right-minded thoughts and aligning the competitiveness in him with the real reason for being on the golf course to begin with.

The Holy Spirit teaches us often through our friends, especially when we play. This is what Jesus meant for us to understand when He spoke of "watching the children play." The Holy Spirit's teaching takes only one direction and has only one goal. His direction is freedom, and His goal is truth. When we have learned that our free will is God's Will, we will feel the freedom and pure joy, and we will be able to relax. If you are denying yourself this, you are denying yourself the Oneness of Heaven.

When Jesus stated, "All power and glory are yours because the Kingdom is His," this is what He really meant, regardless of the ego's interpretation: The Will of God is without limit, and all power and glory are within you, because within you is the Kingdom. It's not located somewhere "out there." It is boundless in its strength, and its love, and its peace. It has no boundaries because it extends within your mind to within the whole Sonship. It is not a physical location where you can go. Please take the physical meaning out of any thoughts you may have of Heaven. If you can do this, the Kingdom of Heaven will come to you. It is yours. What is meant for you will find you.

Your Guide and Communicator knows and sees the truth within you, and in me, and then brings to each of us automatically an acknowledgment of oneness. You will sense it when you accept total truth about everything and allow it to be what it is in everything you do. That's about the best I can explain how I discovered my own freedom, even while being physically behind bars in a state prison. Once this happens for you as it has for me, you will bring your own acknowledgment of it to everyone you encounter. This will be so, because when you accept the truth, you acknowledge everyone as wholly part of God's Will. We can call this a blessing, if you will.

This does not mean you should parade around town announcing it or take out an ad in the newspaper. Those you encounter will sense it and sense it in you. How they sense it for themselves is up to them in their own natural way. This is how truth "works."

When you recognize this, you awaken truth in others automatically, and through their truth you will continue to extend. This is the Atonement process at work.

Chapter 40

Accept It So You Can Give It

Everyone you see around you is blessed due to the certainty of our oneness with all that is real. But if the world is illusory, how do we ever know this to be true? We are able to learn it, and see it clearly, through logic. The Holy Spirit uses logic, just as the ego does. But the Holy Spirit's methods we can understand, and these methods are not insane. The Holy Spirit and the ego take opposite directions. The ego points to untruths, darkness, and death. Death is what keeps the ego motivated and is why it strives for everything quickly and anxiously, before it's too late. We said earlier that the ego sees itself in the space between birth and death. That's why its logic is to "work hard now so you can enjoy life later."

The world has accepted the ego's logic since time began; this is why we continue to fight one war after another. In fact, this logic is what began the clock ticking. Even within ourselves, the battles seem never-ending over time. You would think that by now we would see the ego's logic as not suited for what we truly desire. Let's begin now to turn away from this illusion that only leads us to dust, and instead follow the simple logic by which the Holy Spirit teaches. His lessons through our right-minded thoughts are the simple conclusions that speak for truth, which is all that is real. What logic can this be?

In case you are not aware that you are blessed, please realize that this is of the truth He teaches. The knowledge itself cannot be taught, but because you already have it, it can be realized. You too can learn to bless, but you can't give what you feel you do not have. When you offer a blessing you must first offer it to yourself. What is a blessing, you might ask? It's certainly not a magic trick, performed by putting on some special garments and waving your hand over another's head or by sprinkling some water into a crowd from a pulpit. It is accepting within yourself nothing but the truth and allowing others to witness this about you, as we discussed in the previous section. When others sense the truth in you, they see it in themselves. It may be brief, and they might deny it, but they will know what it is they are denying. In this, they have been blessed *through* you.

If you can't accept your blessedness first in yourself, then how can you give it away by extending it? If the truth you accept for yourself is your own complete forgiveness of your errors, then you will become free of guilt. Your errors are errors of learning, due to the conditioning of the ego. The Holy Spirit cannot undo your errors until after you have made them, and this completed correction may take a little time. During this time period the door to truth will swing open, but the Holy Spirit may have to use an indirect approach that may *seem* frightening and painful.

Just as you are aware in the back of your mind of the speed limit while driving along the interstate highway, also be aware that you have two thought systems to choose from: the real or the unreal. The choice of how you see the world is always within your awareness, and it can help you to see through pain and loss. The experiences of pain and loss are usually perceived as something about you that has failed. The proper thought system enables you to look at this condition as the vehicle that will transcend you into your next highest center. Consider viewing the person experiencing negative feelings and a poor attitude as *troubled*. The individual wonders where he has gone wrong. While ruled by the ego, we work hard at protecting ourselves from discomfort; the experience of pain means that we failed.

Spiritual teachers from many eras, faiths, and perspectives have viewed pain not as a bad thing to be avoided, but more as an inevitable necessity for growth to full spiritual maturity. This spiritual interpretation of pain can have many names. Some have called it "the void." Saint John of the Cross, in the fifteenth century, called it "the dark night of the soul." However you choose to refer to it, one experiences it as the period of time that arrives *between* "what was" and the present's question of "what's next." Within its darkness it has no boundaries and no landmarks. When you're inside it, you feel there will be no end.

Fortunately, there are many survivors who have journeyed through the "void" and emerged more vital, more integrated, more connected to real-life possibilities—not despite, but because of the experience, and because once in it they accepted and welcomed the experience. The void is, after all, perhaps the most effective place for the reordering of one's true thought system to take place, for this is the place where one is least invested in the structures that once circumscribed meaning in one's life.

For instance, I am convinced that my current incarceration is the "dark night of my soul," so to speak. Imprisonment in any fashion surely is a "dark void," and it is that place I write to you from now. Who knows when it will end? When it ends for me, I may not have these same thoughts within me to share that I offer to you now. After my incarceration my future books, talks, and magazine articles will be of the same light, but will perhaps be portrayed with different thoughts.

The indirect method the Holy Spirit uses brings out the truth that was always there within us, in a world made of denial and without direction. When we deny the truth, it is simply a decision not to know. This is why the logic of the world leads to nothing: because its goal is nothing. To have and to give, and still be nothing but a dream, directs you into oblivion. If you strive to have and to be everything, while denying truth, then your chosen thought system is closed off and wholly separate from truth. For this reason, God placed His Holy Spirit in you, where you placed the dream.

In your dream of separation, you see everything as being outward. With this vision, if your thoughts were one hundred percent wholly of yourself, then the thought system you chose to make up would be forever dark. The Holy Spirit makes light available always, but in the darkness any thoughts you do share with God are transmuted beyond your ego-based belief. If you will learn to inwardly extend these thoughts that you do share with God, without fear, you will begin to see the power in your thoughts.

So far, it has been the ego-based projections of the world, and not the truth, that you have chosen to defend and think that you love. Remember, we discussed that images are projected, and real thoughts extend. No one can take these thoughts away from you; however, you can give them up. Your Source of undoing these projections that lead to your errors is within you, and is the One who knows everything about you.

If the Holy Spirit's thought system is not leading you, then the direction of your life will go nowhere and will find nothing. If you deny something that He well knows to be true, then He must teach you not to deny it. The Holy Spirit's undoing is always over time and is indirect as you involve yourself in the task of trying to share with God that which cannot be shared, but merely needs correction. This is where you could possibly, for a temporary period of time, enter the "void," or "the dark night of the soul," as Saint John of the Cross named it. (By the way, upon further reading up on Saint John of the Cross, I discovered that he seemed to be one who thought against the norm, one of whom others said his ideas were "a bit wild." But I didn't learn what, back in those days, was considered to be wild!)

You must understand how twisted and fragmented and complex mankind's thought system is, given the multiple generations of illusion, lies, untruths, and false love passed down to us. The Holy Spirit must begin His teaching by showing you what you can never learn on your own, especially from the world. His message sometimes might come directly at you, where He must introduce truth to insanity. In such cases—as it did with my incarceration— His direct message can force you into complete surrender. He may look at your foundation and dismiss it, but you yourself cannot undo what you made.

Whether His correction is direct or indirect, His undoing will start a rebuilding, though it may seem for quite a while as though you are stuck and going nowhere. For me, it felt like He took a wrecking ball to my life, but then said to me, "It's okay, let it rest, and now I will help you to rebuild, and it will be something fascinating." The time will come when you suddenly see yourself traveling with simple truths and notice a burst of real positive progression. This is what has given me the energy to write this book while in a state prison.

The ancient Chinese *Book of Changes*, or *I Ching*, speaks of such a life experience being like water filling up behind the wall of a dam. From the other side of the dam, it can look like absolutely nothing is happening. Then all it takes is one last drop to cause the pooling water to rise over the top and become a rushing river, effortlessly flowing into the next stage of its journey.

Chapter 41

Looking Beyond with Your Christ Vision

No one knows better than myself that I was on the receiving end of some terrible legal advice, which sent me to prison. But I've gotten over it. I am aware that I'm not alone—far from it. This happens to many who have never experienced the criminal justice system. It has been said that negotiating for an appropriate prison sentence in a plea bargain can be compared to shopping for a car. In my case, I paid the "sticker price."

With no plea deal, I surrendered myself to the court, riding on my lawyer's lies, in hopes for leniency from both the judge and the prosecutor. The real truth of the matter, which was extremely simple, was covered up, while the facts of my errors should have been presented for an accurate understanding of my case. I was certainly guilty, but not as portrayed by my lawyer's plan, which backfired. I became lost as I contemplated the ten-year prison term slammed down hard by the gavel. The ride back to jail from the courthouse—chained, shackled, and handcuffed in the back of the paddy wagon—at least gave me some time to tell myself that the long, enduring court process was now behind me. Regardless of the pain and loss I felt, I was able to look ahead at what might be in the cards for me with prison. This was extremely frightening, but something in me was welcoming it. Some say this welcoming a prison sentence was due to relief that the trial was over and I had survived. But all along and ever since, I've chosen not to see it that way.

During that grueling time, I did not receive a single visit at the county jail, nor did any member of my large family show up at the sentencing. I surely could have used an ear to bend in sorting things out. I later would find out they were "too busy" and had "lives of their own." I could only think about how I must have shamed them, because I was certainly ashamed of myself. I also thought maybe their nonsupport was a payback for something I may have done, or not done, in my past. My own daughters were humiliated by my selfish acts that had proven to be felonies. Their father was now a convicted felon, and I would carry that image for the remainder of my life.

My self-berating continued. It was later said that my lawyer took advantage of my inexperience with the "business" of criminal justice and used me as a trade-off for another one of his clients caught up in a drug-dealing crime. It seems there was more hard cash in that deal. I now found myself hating myself, my lawyer, and the judicial system. I was deep in a hole, and there was no one available to throw me a rope. If there had been, I might have used the rope to hang myself.

But my whole point in the small scenario I just relived for you is to display how this pity-party thought system I chose to use was made in my mind. It's all true and nothing is exaggerated, except possibly the "hanging rope" part. I was highly disappointed in my family, but whatever reasons they had for not showing up were not in my control, nor was it up to me to try to own their feelings. But soon, and I mean very soon, for whatever reason I still cannot explain today, something started tugging on me inside and telling me through strong thoughts that I was not alone and it was okay, and that I needed to stop the condemning of everyone, including myself—especially myself.

Although physically I was alone, there was a small friendly fire gently burning inside me, calm like a campfire, that urged me to relax. The abuse I was giving myself had to stop, and it did. I had no special training in this; I simply settled down and felt centered on getting through this experience, and beginning a new life. Something encouraged me to keep my focus for a while on the judge's comment about my ten-year prison term being "non-mandatory." I began asking myself, "What does this mean?" My lawyer had never bothered to explain. This was the only rope I had to hang on to—more like a string—but it was enough. What I didn't realize at that time was that total surrender was forced on me, with the thought of a non-mandatory sentence granting me some relief from the tight chains that held me. This was a part of the undoing process that had been going on all along. Although I did not realize this at the time, it seemed as though I began forgiving myself.

Material truth entails conforming with ideas the world justifies as its own, or something it wants to govern. There was nothing at all material in the truth I found in forgiving myself. I am talking about inner truth, where spirit abides, the only place true forgiveness can come from. The ego can never understand this. It's also impossible to ever know inner truth while being unforgiving and condemning at the same time.

My turn away from the ego toward right-minded truth developed quite indirectly, but my surrender seemed dramatic and direct. Amazingly, now I can see that the most truthful thing I had done at that point was to accept the fact that I had already been judged, and that all judgment over me regarding my material errors was now a thing of the past. But there remained a part of me that was still judging and condemning myself, taking me on an emotional roller coaster ride. The steep slow inclines felt comfortable with acceptance of a new beginning, but the fast downslopes stared right into the teeth of ten years in prison. Still looking "out there" for someone or something to grant me further forgiveness, I was looking at a long, long ride.

Then I encountered the nurse who checked me over a few days later, taking my vital signs before I was to be chained, shackled, and handcuffed, and loaded onto a bus for prison. She was aware of my ordeal, being that my case had been plastered all over the local papers, including a rude statement by a reporter saying I was "brought to my knees." Everyone in the entire county jail, including inmates, had read the story and knew I was going away for a long time. As the nurse had her fingers on my pulse, she kindly whispered into my right ear an encouraging message. "You seem like a nice man. You simply made a mistake and didn't hurt anyone. Just forgive yourself; it'll be okay." Her kind words sunk in immediately, and I'll never forget the loving expression on her face as I looked over my shoulder at her while the deputy escorted me off to the transport area.

Her reassurance also gave me the sense to see that I was free from being judged further. Her effortless gesture at a time of my despair told me that I was the only one who could do the forgiving, and not an outside source, or an idol, or a man dressed in black with a white collar, or ritual words on a piece of paper that are hard to understand, or anything else that claims outside power or magic. Nothing but the truth within me could ever know about the "overlooking by looking beyond" that I needed to do. To rely on an idol to grant you forgiveness or strength only prevents the truth that is within you from being known. This makes you wish to find forgiveness outside yourself, where it does not exist. The power of God is within you, because it is you. This is why your completeness cannot be given to you by something *out there*.

I hope my story here reflects your own awareness of the Holy Spirit in you, and the happenings in your own life. It is your awareness of His presence that may have been missing when you may have faced despair or turmoil. You can begin to strengthen this awareness as you strengthen your alertness. Many of us have been caught up in the world of perception, which means we are caught up in finding an answer that exists outside of us. But an idol is a wrong-minded remedy of the ego, whose only strength is that it can get you to perceive the way it wants you to. It points "out there" where *nothing* knows the real you.

The only true help is your True Helper, which is in all of us. He is housed in your right-mind and watches over you as you dream of a life of time and space. He will, upon your invitation, arbitrate between the pull of the ego on you and true reality. All of us at one time or another have experienced some intuition and dismissed it as luck or a whim. But was it really a whim? It is you, along with the Holy Spirit, that brings about any such luck. These aspects within you that the Holy Spirit reveals, including Him, are the vision of the Christ-Mind completed. This is your wholeness reflected as your strength, rather than the weaknesses you experience on the fast downslopes.

I must go further to say that if you listen to these intuitions or sensations of truth, you will find the Holy Spirit will give you what you need for your growth at that moment—even if it is only a tiny wisp of strength that seems to be holding on by a thread, such as my own thoughts of a "non-mandatory" prison term, meaning hope for an early release or parole. That's all I had, but somehow that thought was given to me, as well as the strength to hold onto it. The ego through its wrong-mindedness might argue and say that the thought of an early release was only a survival instinct—a delusion. Yes, this may be true, but there's more beyond this that the ego can never recognize. To that, the ego may respond that this is insane or preposterous or arrogant. But that's just like the ego—always attacking when it doesn't know what to do next. The truth is that I was given a path to hope, like a ray of light, that led me out of the depths of despair and allowed me to see the face of Christ in my desperate surroundings. When the hope for early release fell away, I was still left standing in the light. But without that slender hope at that time, none of my right-mind would have been available to fulfill my purpose in the Sonship.

That hope was essential because it kept me from succumbing to my deepest despair imaginable—a subjective state we experience when our inner resources are sufficient to cope with a situation. I was able, by a thread of hope at my innermost core, to avoid a meltdown of the trust I had in myself to endure this period in my life: a prison term of ten years. Fortunately, my dad always taught me to keep moving toward the goal, and my mother was always matter-of-fact. Thanks to that early guidance,

I've never totally lost sight of the knowledge that the universe—the working of the whole—is always on my side. My strength has used time to rebuild. Oh sure, my weaknesses still sneak up on me in the form of anxiety. But with the Christ-Mind as my thought system, I will continue to endure.

The Christ vision is put together by the Holy Spirit and communicated to us through Him. Did I recognize the face of Christ in the nurse? As well, did she in me? And let's not forget that when you are able to notice or spot the sneaky little tricks of the ego, either in yourself or in others, you are doing so with Christ vision. When you see the ego's trickery you will know to acknowledge it only for the nothingness that it is, and move quickly on to your next thought.

Forgiveness is the means to keep spirit alive, and through forgiveness the thinking of the world is reversed. How is this so? you may ask. Because forgiveness is overlooking the ego and looking beyond it. This is why forgiveness is the necessary correction for all errors. If you have not forgiven yourself about something that has been bothering you, then the ego in you still rules over you. If the ego in you is governing you, how can you forgive others? If this is the case, you are doing the Atonement process no good. So do yourself some right-minded good by going within and throwing out the ego. You do this by realizing the truth. It will become automatic, and you'll find it catching on with others with whom you interact.

This doesn't take much time at all, nor does it require special penance, which the ego will try to trick you into. But beware, the ego may accuse you of being in denial. Simply disregard any such antics, and ask the Holy Spirit, from your own inner knowledge of truth, to accept your errors. He will undo them quickly, and you will start witnessing the changes. Is this denial? It certainly is. It's called "denying the ego the right to be real in your life."

Chapter 42

The Fear of What You've Always Been

The darkness of the world can be summed up as the infiltration of the ego; not necessarily evil, just simply wrong-minded erroneous thinking. Through wrong-minded thinking we bring the same type of perception to others. The ego projects itself outward and is determined to survive until its bitter end. However, there are many of us who strive to bring darkness to the light. We can heal the split-mind by putting out darkness in this way, thereby building a solid foundation in the essence of humanity as a whole. We are lifting the veil that has been observing the face of Christ, where we can see ourselves in truth, and where sin, and the guilt that made it, no longer exist.

The question for you is: Are you willing to do what it takes to see a reality that never had sin to begin with, and to live with peace and joy, free of guilt? This does not entail sacrifice at all. Or do you wish to live your life under dark clouds that limit you in your true purpose? I realize there are those who say that the body is real, and that it is all there is to life, that when the body dies, "It's over—that's it, lights out." Whatever way you choose to live, only you know within yourself whether or not you are living a life that fulfills your purpose. Only this is your true free will.

No matter how you decide to view this cloud cover, whatever excuses you come up with, you indeed know if you are lost or not. You may say things to yourself such as, "I'm just waiting for the economy to turn around" or "Once the kids get through college I'll be able to free up more time." We've been taught and programmed to always be looking "out there" for that "someday" that we wish to believe is the magic pill. Would you dare to consider these excuses as a cop out to your fear of your own ego's anger toward you? This is being afraid of your own shadow. Out of fear, you simply do not wish to rebel against the ego. If for some time, before even reading this book, you have been sensing what I'm discussing here, then this is the Holy Spirit's Voice touching you. Of course, any fear you have is an illusory front of the ego, designed to scare you. If you're finding what I'm saying hard to believe, then ask the Truth that is inside you what it is you are denying. Simply ask, "How do I truly choose to live?"

In his book *The Power of Now*, spiritual leader and psychologist Eckhart Tolle describes what he calls a "critical-limit situation." This caught my attention due to my own personal disaster, drastic upheaval, deep loss, and suffering. A critical-limit situation occurs when an individual's whole world is shattered, turned upside-down, and doesn't make sense anymore. It is an encounter with death, be it physical or psychological. It is not the "void" we discussed in a previous section, but it is the shock that can send one into the "dark night of the soul," as Saint John of the Cross named it.

In a critical-limit situation, the ego-based mind that made yourself and your own world collapses. It appears that much of the world—individuals and nations alike—will need a critical-limit situation to spur us to recognize the undoing process by the Holy Spirit; forcing us to surrender and enter into an awakened state that starts with right-mindedness. This is the only way to move on up to One-mindedness; the right-mind gets us there. There is no guarantee, of course, that even this type of situation will do it, because humankind is stuck so deeply in wrong-mindedness, but our potential is there. Some will never recognize this, however, and merely wither away.

Please be assured that it's not necessary to wait until you suffer a big fall or collapse to accept the One mind; but if you do, there is only one way to get up. I believe you are aware of this, and this is why you have reached this far into this book at this particular time in your life.

With my own experience of near psychological death, more than anyone could ever imagine or understand, rather than wither, something took hold of me within and said, "Get up, you'll be okay. Come on, let's move on," and rebuilding began. I don't have to try to make anyone understand, nor do I have a need to explain the details, unless I'm asked and it may help someone else find their way.

A whole new picture has been presented to me, and it's of a world that's now in my heart. It's good enough for me. These effects on me had a *cause*, and they are also *effects* on the whole Sonship. I am constantly amazed by the messages I receive from the Holy Spirit through other individuals, who most often don't even realize the message passing through them and on to me. If not already, I believe you will start to see and hear the same type of messages for yourself. In order for you to master your own spiritual freedom, you must overcome a hurdle, after which you will automatically recognize His communication throughout your day-to-day life. For crystal-clear communication with the Universal Communicator, you must be able to operate in every moment of your life from the memory of God. That's right, you will need to remember God. Your separated thought system obscures your true vision, and when faced with the real world you clam up because of fear. So let's get over this hurdle by first asking yourself a question you need to honestly absorb, and then giving yourself a truthful answer.

Is it more difficult for you to say "I love" than "I hate?"

In households all around the world, many families are shy or not acculturated to say "I love you" regularly. It's as though we are supposed to assume love, but saying the word should be reserved for a time when needed the most. The world has taught us to associate love with weakness, and hatred with strength. We are taught that our power comes from having to "prove" ourselves, making us feel strong, or stronger.

When you have a joyous or loving response to an individual or a situation, do you still feel the need to prove yourself further? Perhaps you tell yourself that you cannot continue to process these joyous and loving thoughts for too long, because the entire world you think you made for yourself could vanish or be lost. You tell yourself, "There's been enough love and fun, but now I must get real," or you say with strength, "The party's over and now it's time to get serious." Does any of this sound familiar?

You might believe in the idols the world has taught you about or insist that "pain is the way to gain" and "too much" joy or pleasure can be a deterrent. You will, then, leave your joy and love behind for a while until you believe you have endured the appropriate amounts of pain. You may think that if you continue to give, you will be leading yourself to loss, and you have already sacrificed and worked hard to earn what you have built. But the ego in you will get defensive and say, "So? What's wrong with hard work?" Does this sound familiar?

In this disordered state of mind, it is not your trumped-up fears that you are mostly afraid of. Your real terror is having freedom from your ego, because it has been your comfort zone. But what if it were stripped from you or taken away? This, of course, happens in the death of your body, because the ego is of your body. But what about inner psychological death, where everything you were about is now gone? Now your own fear does not know what to fear, but it is still afraid. Why is this?

Because without the ego, or very minimal ego, our wrong-mindedness has no backbone, and we think this is what we truly are. The illusions no longer mean anything, and we feel there is nothing left to gain. This can indeed seem momentarily terrifying—as if we are rootless and untethered. Of course the ego is still in you; it has merely been silenced. But now, with this silence, the memory of God shines through. It is the memory of what you were before your physical birth. It is the memory of what rests behind the dream of separation. It is what we always have been all along: *pure knowledge*. It's strong because it's true. Have you ever had the honest and true sensation that there must be a better way? If your answer is yes, then you know the memory of God. The love and truth within you is what you are in reality.

This memory will instantly restore you to your proper place, when all along it has been the place you've been trying to leave. What's happening here is that the little bit of ego remaining within you is fearful of your True Self, which is God. The dwindling ego doesn't know how to handle this. You have been under the influence of ego-based thought for so long, you're not aware of the fact that the real you doesn't need this wrong-minded way of seeing things. Your ego begins seeing that it no longer will dominate by being able to purchase strength with *material muscle*. As you have just now read this, you will have one of two reactions. You may give a slight chuckle or laugh in a sarcastic fashion, which is the ego trying to hang on by a string. Or the Christ in you is in awe with a *knowing* of this to be true.

Our fear of attack is nothing compared to our fear of love. In a near psychological death as I just described, there is nothing to attack because nothing remains, only God, which is not going to attack. Only the ego will, through yourself, such as the self-berateing and abuse I initiated in myself. But the Holy Spirit stands by and watches over this, and He then turns it around and uses everything He can to undo the errors that you made. For a while this may make you even more fearful, because you're sensing that God, or yourself-in-truth, is all that remains of you. But at that point, you don't realize that that was all you ever needed. The Oneness that you are is beginning to be aware of Itself. Can we say that "The house that burns down will be rebuilt better than it ever was before?"

Chapter 43

Bringing It All to Him

This world of separated thought has helped us to teach ourselves that the way to gain salvation is to attack and to fight for something. Throughout history we have been fighting to save ourselves from something, and to this day that "something" still holds us prisoner. We are quite simply our own jailer, and if we cannot—equally simply—"let go" of this power struggle, we will continue to see God as attacking our empires. The prayers seem to pour out with accusations and requests, such as "Oh my God, what did I do to deserve this?" or "Please vanquish my enemies (that I might gain)," or "How much more do you want to take from me?" This is so because we see the illusory location of God as "out there" and as a threat to the wrong-mindedness we believe comforts us. We must realize that this "no space" or "spaceless" location we occupy is God. There is nothing "out there" except your body that you made from a fantasy thought. A "bite into an apple" that projected more than it really was. A simple error in thought. Nothing sinful about it.

There is nothing for God to take control over, because He is what we are, which is total love. There is no space needed to house love. This is why we are often afraid of our own potential: When we can accept this, the love of God within us seems to pour out. But we've been believing that our salvation lies in trying to prove ourselves faithful to a "ruler" or a "king" high above. This perception makes us defensive; we fear the version of an "outside God's" love, which makes us feel little and governed by such a ruler, when all along we are this ruler to ourselves. Remember, our true free will is God's Will.

We have been using the world and trying to hide the fact that we do indeed possess this love, and want to show it all the time. Look around you at the striving for attention that is everywhere. This is why we still wish to hold onto the ego's dark foundation as a secure place to hide our love, and only bring it out when there's something to gain. We use hate as our weapon to protect this foundation. This is where we think our safety rests, and this is why it's easier for us to hate those "others" "out there." The ego thinks it portrays strength. But this illusory dark foundation has been reinforcing its structure with illusion upon illusion, ever since that loving couple looked to that shiny apple on the "Tree of Life." This reinforcing of its cornerstone called "the false idea of what we are" has nothing to do with eternity, but it does have everything to do with *wasting time.*

It's easy for us to accept this insanity because we made it ourselves, through the lessons taught to us by our idols, and what we make we "take pride in." But we find it difficult to accept and give love, because we were not taught to make it. Why? Because even the ego in us is aware that love cannot be made. It was created, and love is what it is, just as truth is—real and unlimited. There are no specially designed sets of plans on how to create love. In fact, the ego covers its face when it sees us trying to "make love" and discourages the sight of any such love. Love was given to us to be shared and not earned. What is shared will extend, and what extends becomes one.

A Course in Miracles teaches us that "Our individual death seems more valuable than our living oneness, for what is given us is not so dear as what we made." This is merely the *Course's* attempt to open our eyes. Doesn't it seem as though we are more afraid of love than we are of the ego? The point here is that love cannot enter where it's not welcome. But hatred can, and will force its way, not caring at all for the real you.

You certainly do care for yourself, however; and since the Holy Spirit is in you, He certainly cares for you. With this acceptance, here's what you can do. Go ahead, right now, and with all that love that is in you, take any and all suffering you have incurred, and the hatred you are confronted with, or possess in yourself, and bring it to the altar in your right-mind for the Holy Spirit to view. Picture yourself standing there, as one with Him, regarding all that sits before this Oneness. Ask that this mess be cleared away and brought back as something great.

This does not require that you get on your knees for any length of time, nor do you need to light special candles, blow on a special horn, nor do you need to have special beads, water, or oils. Not a single ceremony or ritual is required. Simply take a few short, honest moments, with straight talk or even merely a thought, and know in your heart that your plea is backed up with the truth and love that you were created from. He is your Guide, and He will help you as your Friend, because your success is necessary for the entire Sonship. He wants you to complete your part in the Atonement.

Hidden beneath all the grandiosity the world has praised you for, or even stomped on you for, is your real call for help. Remember that your call for help through the Universal Healer, which is connected to God, is not a call to a location *out there*. That place outside of you can only offer an idol to praise. God does not need praising, because He has no ego that needs stroking. It all happens within you. You are the Idea of His Thought, therefore His Thought is you. This One Thought that you are did not make all the suffering in your world. God doesn't punish us, because this would be punishing ourselves. Your own separated thought, which you made and continue to dream of, believes in the world's own separated thought. You simply demanded that it happen. Your demands brought the thought forward.

Whenever you find yourself clinging to hatred rather than love, or feeling love as a form of weakness, use the following words in the form of a prayer:

> I cannot fail when I stick like glue to the truth.
>
> The truth is never weak. It makes me strong.
>
> The power in any decision is my own, given to me by God.

Chapter 44

There Is Nothing Else beyond Truth

In order that we may live our own true free will, we must minimize ego-based contributions to our own wrong-mindedness. As long as we are here on this planet in the dream of time and space, we cannot be totally ego-free, but we can silence the ego to the point where it holds no weight in our daily living. To do this, the Holy Spirit needs us to be a "happy learner."

We already discussed that you must lay all your cards on the table for the Holy Spirit to see. Of course He already knows the cards you hold, but He needs to see how you present this to Him. The way you display truth to the Holy Spirit helps Him to determine the methods of His operation for the undoing of your errors that led you here. You have been directed by the world to believe that one day your misery will lead to happiness, and your True Guide must reinterpret this for you.

The world has confused us into believing that we can do anything we set our minds on doing. The missing link has been determining what we truly want and which side of our split-mind is doing the learning. Without considering this carefully, and receiving the Right Guidance, misery will continue to find more misery.

I literally drove myself into madness with excessive wrong-minded perceptions and thinking, entailing excessive working hours, leading to excessive "happy hours," leading to excessive personal problems that ultimately led me to excessive darkness. Is this an excuse? No. It is what it is, a series of errors in thought, by using the wrong thought system to run my life. I was working hard at not enjoying a pathway I wrong-mindedly thought was paved for success. Never realizing my *true* free will, and not understanding I was merely building a foundation for nothingness, I continued to value the hard work as a necessary part of the formula for success. The world awarded me with the pleasures my ego deserved. It all made sense, I thought.

We converse with countless other egos that counsel faith in our hard work, even when it leads to misery. "Be patient," we are told. "Keep on keeping on." After all, "No pain, no gain" and "Rome wasn't built in a day." What these other egos don't speak of, however—only because they don't know themselves—is that if we have faith in *nothing*, then we will always value *nothing*. Anything outside of yourself is this "nothing" I'm talking about. If we continue to value what is outside of us, then we are in the "nothing business." If we're attempting this type of business, then we are attempting to make the untrue into something that is true. This is the false idea of a free will that the ego likes to waste time over.

If you are in a place where you don't belong, the Holy Spirit wants you to see truth is truly where you belong. What is not true in your life at this moment is never going to suddenly, or even gradually, make itself be true. Time does not make the truth, but it can help you to see it. This only seems like a hard lesson to learn, because your ego and others may think otherwise, and fight you on it. But all you need do for now is to simply consider all the distortions you have made of nothing, and the strange forms and feelings, actions and reactions that you weave of the falsities in your life. Be truthful on this with yourself, and don't worry about having to share this with any other individual, unless you choose to. There really is nothing to dissect, or have long deep thought over when it comes to understanding truth. It cannot be understood; it can only be accepted. To try and dissect it is only your fight against it.

By your willingness to be what you are intended to be, which is what you truly want, you must trust that the Universal Inspiration will inspire you to release your sights from the nothingness you have been living by. As the darkness you have been living under is drawn to the Light, all others will begin seeing this change in you, and the Sonship will know it. People will start showing up in your life to assist you with your loving purpose. Everyone you encounter will notice the light about you, and they will see in you what you have not been seeing in yourself. Some will be cautious at first. However, this is necessary so that their curiousness may be exposed to your light, which will bring them to eventually being a "happy learner" as well, in some fashion that complements their uniqueness. After all, isn't this how you are becoming a happy learner?

Keep in mind that the Holy Spirit did not create truth. It always has been and will always be. Therefore, when you extend truth through your ever-radiant light, you are continuing to learn from the Holy Spirit as it flows from God. As you begin to hear the Holy Spirit coming through other happy learners, the lesson will always remain that we will never be able to make nothing into everything. This lesson in itself is strong enough to keep the ego silenced. You will see that nothingness has previously been your goal, and now you have let go of this foolishness. The foolishness is constantly being corrected and reversed, and then given back to you as Truth.

In myself, I started noticing that I didn't worry any longer over the shame I once felt for being labeled a "convicted felon" and for the grief I caused my family. I accepted the fact that their thoughts were their own. I do not own or control anyone else's thoughts. When I now write letters to them from prison, I overlook (forgive) any such thoughts they may have. I focus my communication to them on my own optimism in that my errors are now behind me, and for now while still in prison, I am okay. My focus is on what I am doing now, and not on what has already gone by. This, in turn, allows me to be more concerned with them.

In your case it may involve overlooking the grumpiness in your spouse, and understanding that it is from the ego, and not giving it any of your own ego-based feedback. This does not mean that you should stay in an abusive relationship, of course; but only you would know if it is time to move on. Remember, by overlooking now, by looking beyond ego-based behavior, your spouse will see to forgive you when it is the appropriate time. Merely having a radiant, firm glow about your attitude throughout the household, no matter who is complaining, can show the love in you. This doesn't mean you need to be all smiles or "peachy" every moment of the day. Nor does it mean adopting an "I'm holier than you" attitude toward your grumpy spouse. This would be the ego kicking in once again, suggesting a separation between you, rather than oneness in the Face of Christ. It simply means truly loving.

This radiance you carry can also be in your own seriousness when a firm stance needs to be taken. This is where the truth may need to be pushed forward. There is nothing nonspiritual about giving a firm "no" when you feel it necessary. This could be in your pointing to the box of laundry detergent in a firm but loving fashion when your teenager demands clean laundry for the third time this week. You could smile, while firmly stating that it's time she learns to do her own laundry. She will most likely start requiring fewer loads of clean laundry. Wouldn't you agree?

When you see any discomfort in anyone, you will automatically know that it's coming from "nothing," and you will know from within yourself how to respond *without* reacting. If and when you feel such discomfort dwelling inside of you, simply stop for a moment and acknowledge it for what it is. In my book *The Master of Everything*, I called this procedure using your "spiritual flashlight" to shine your light onto those dark-clouded feelings. Notice them for the nothingness they are, and they will fade away by being drawn into your light. Then you can move on to the right-mindedness you truly are all about. Putting your own radiant light to the wrong-mindedness will keep you moving along your own spiritual path.

The nothingness you have been living by is not what you want. Jesus once said, "Be not content with nothing." The world has perpetuated the belief for centuries that nothing can give us everything. Remember what you have learned, now that you realize there is "another way of looking at the world."

To be a happy learner you must give everything to your True Helper to be unlearned and reinterpreted for you. Then you can begin to learn the joyous lessons that will come quickly to you, as the new firm foundation that your truth will build for you. You will see that truth is actually true and is nothing else. The universe of learning will open itself up for you, so that all that was intended of God's Will for you, in simple fashion, will be yours. It will be yours because it has always been your true free will. With all of this as your Home, you will not have a need to look at the past.

Once your vision is of this Light, you will have met the conditions of Oneness. The learning will continue for as long as time and space remain with us, because it's needed, for now, so that the Holy Spirit can help silence the ego with quiet and calm inspiration. The Holy Spirit, which is your True Self, has now freed you from the past. Always remember that the Communicator of all of time and space is the Truth that you are. The most important dimension for you now, of course, is your own internal process of undoing all that obscures your awareness of Love's presence. With this new clear vision, you have started mastering your own spiritual freedom.

Afterword

When I first discovered the dirty, yellowed, nicotine-stained, battered, and torn copy of *A Course in Miracles* on a scrappy prison library shelf, I knew I was being sent a gift. This thought struck me due to the feeling I'd had for quite a few years that a positive change in me was needed. My churning confusion had gotten the best of me. The timing was appropriate when the message rang through me that I was no longer alone or lacking. Abundance was merely waiting for me to open my eyes. I heard mention of *A Course in Miracles* periodically and at odd times during my business years, as I would read the books of certain self-help authors. I intended to look further and it was totally unlike me not to, but something always seemed to hold me back.

In my previous book, *The Master of Everything*, I describe this miracle meeting in detail, and I've written this book as its follow-up message. I wasted no time diving into the extremely deep content the *Course* offers, and although I have always been an avid reader, I found its subject matter to be like a foreign language: difficult to understand and to contemplate. But Truth does ring through its depth.

I found that after extended periods of reading the text, I would often get headaches, watery and burning eyes, and my nerves would feel on edge, leading to frustration and anxiety. I would become cranky or grouchy and feel defensive, snapping at and berating myself over the slightest things, which were usually a result of reliving my past. This was not a good attitude for my survival in prison, where I thought I needed to be as sharp as a tack.

Later I would learn and accept these reactions as my own ego in revolt against me, a resistance to the Oneness of mind I was shifting toward. It was my ego's fight over losing control of my real self, which it thought had been trapped and bound. I find this no different than when you put a baby down at bedtime who screams in rage, throwing a tantrum over not wanting to go to sleep. But by keeping the child in bed and ignoring its tirade, the child's antics with time will simmer down, and with the use of more time the child goes to sleep.

The urging swelled in me to dive deeper, to absorb like a sponge all that I could of the *Course's* many volumes of text, workbook for students, and manual for teachers. Still difficult to comprehend on the surface, something was directing and leading me to keep on reading, regardless of what I did not understand initially. I was loving the process as it pulled me deeper, and the urging voice was constant for me to continue.

The more I got involved, the more I knew there was no returning. I would become unnerved easily, and unsettled over simple sentences in the text that were totally opposite of what I'd been taught as a child. Wild dreams plagued me regularly at night, often scary and grotesque, with images that haunted me. One recurring nightmare in particular gave me images of a sea of floating heads, bobbing up against one another, frantically questioning one another over the predicament they were in. I needed desperately to get to the shore, but my rowboat would not budge any further, with wave after wave of floating heads banging against my boat, all crying out for help. They wanted me to help them.

I didn't know what to do, and my only choice would be to get out of the boat and walk on top of the heads to the shore, which appeared to be miles away. I would always seem to come out of the dream just before stepping out of the boat. I would lose sleep trying to analyze it, and worry myself over it the next day. I could barely remember any meaning or plot to many of the other dreams, but it was clear they were frightening. My ego was threatened as it felt itself slowing fading into my Light. The ego was covering its eyes to the radiant glow the words from the text of the *Course* were starting to extend into me. Or, we could say the real me was overriding ego territory, and my ego was trying to order me to *halt*, or else.

But the real part of me was diving deeper and could care less about ego threats, and for that matter had no intention, or a single reason, to fight back. As I continued my journey absorbing the messages of Oneness, Truth, and forgiveness, the dreams continued with more terrifying intensity. I woke up one night in the wee hours, sat up on my top bunk in a cold sweat, and in the overcrowded prison dormitory, among 272 inmates, I screamed out, "Stop it now!" Within time the dreams became weaker and weaker. I still to this day have some crazy dreams occasionally, but now I simply see them as laughable and am able to dismiss them as the unreality they are.

But my ego wasn't giving up that easily. Next, in my own anxiety and foul attitude, it seemed like I was attacking myself further. This would occur especially often following a few hours, or longer, of reading the text. I felt waves of irritability, as though I was being antagonized. One particular section in the manual for teachers showed me why I can never go deep enough, due to the boundary-less, infinite reality of which I am, along with all of the people I meet or run into daily, even in prison, where egos are physically jailed. To question what is enough, or a limit to infinity, merely brings on more conflict.

When questions now hit me, most of the time the answer is suddenly available in my mind. They seem to pop up and be answered quickly, with no effort. At first I would question this quickness of receiving. But soon I would be urged to let go of these doubting thoughts, and instead to accept life calmly with confidence and faith.

There began to be times, and I am noticing them more each day, when I could find a place to sit in peace with a quiet mind that has no ego-based chatter—say, in the prison yard, maybe noticing the oak tree in its changing seasons outside the barbed-wire and double-razor-edged fence. Or I might take in the serene sight of a rainbow in the sky, or a bird or two sitting on the back of a bench, or a hawk hovering overhead. A place where I have no thoughts, only simply noticing. I would begin to see a glow of light, radiant, so to speak, surrounding that object.

Could this be my imagination? a slightly negative thought would ask me. But I would disregard that thought too and, rather, simply enjoy the calmness of the serene beauty I was seeing. I soon decided not to question it any further. To this day when I notice the glow of things, I accept it for what it is, a gift.

There seems to be a mass belief that what we see in the outer world is more important than our inner world. However, I do believe change is beginning to take place in the world. We have had for centuries a mass belief in scarcity in this world, fearing there is not enough for everyone. This is the underlying belief that is the source of competition and power struggles of civilizations throughout history. The same belief causes strife between neighbors. I mean no negative judgment here, but only an observation that some people learn in particular ways that make life difficult for them.

I hope you have started to see that there is another way of looking at the world, and that your individual struggles are with you and you can easily let them go. You may place yourself in the forefront of the projected forms or images of what *you think you are*. From here I hope you can bring to your attention that the mass beliefs by which most individuals live only serve to inhibit spiritual freedom. Once you recognize these beliefs you can choose whether or not you agree with them and want to live by them or not. Life is eternal and so are you and I, and there is nothing to fear. With that thought alone, I hope you look for me up the road.

God bless.

Bibliography

The Foundation for Inner Peace. *A Course in Miracles*. Temecula, CA, 1975.

Coleson, Charles. *The Good Life*. Carol Stream, IL: Tyndale House, 2005.

Covey, Stephen R. *The 8th Habit*. New York: Simon & Schuster, 2006.

Cramor, Kathryn D., Ph.D. *Staying on Top*. New York: Viking Penguin, 1998.

Gandhi, Arun. "Reflections of Peace." Brigham Young University, Provo, UT, *BYU Magazine* 54, no. 1 (Spring 2000).

Leider, Richard J., and David A. Shapiro. *Repacking Your Bags*. New York: MJF Books, 1995.

Maxwell, John C. *The Difference Maker*. Nashville, TN: Thomas Nelson Publishing, 2006.

McArthur, Bruce. *Your Life*. Virginia Beach, VA: A.R.E. Press, 1993.

Orsborn, Carol. *Solved by Sunset*. Nevada City, CA: Harmony Books, 1997.

Pascal, Blaise. *Pensées*. Translated by A. J. Krailisheimer. London: Penguin, 1996.

Pipher, Mary. *The Shelter of Each Other*. New York: Riverhead Books, 2008.

Schuller, Robert. *Success Is Never Ending, Failure Is Never Final*. Nashville, TN: Thomas Nelson, 1988.

Stevens, D. E., and Meher Baba. *Listen Humanity*. New York: Crossroad Publishing, 1971.

Tolle, Eckhart. *The Power of Now*. Novato, CA: New World Library, 1999.

Williamson, Marianne. *A Return to Love*. New York: Harper Collins, 1996.

Witkin, Dr. Georgia. *Passions*. New York: Villard Books, 1992.

World Progress Yearbook. Chicago, IL: Standard Education Corp., 1994.

About the Author

Following tours of duty at Kent State University and in the U.S. Air Force, he spent the next twenty-five years in the financial services industry, excelling in a field he loathed – though not immune to its perks. By his thirties, running his own independent agency, he became an experienced public speaker and wrote a monthly column on financial security for *Senior Forum*, a regional Ohio newsletter. He then launched his own monthly client newsletter, *Retirement Insights*, which became hugely popular and evolved into a self-help publication with a nontraditional, nonreligious, spiritual slant.

Despite a long, successful career, in 2007 – faced with the pressures of an economy in freefall; the loss of one wife to cancer and two to divorce; the needs of his children and demands of an upscale lifestyle; and responsibilities to panicking clients – he illegally withdrew $100,000 of client's funds to try to recoup the value of their investments and rescue his floundering business. The strategy failed and landed him a sentence of ten years.

His time in prison has been hell, and has also been unexpectedly fruitful, resulting in his return to his first love, writing, and the series that begins with *The Master of Everything*. The manuscripts were painstakingly handwritten in lined notebooks (he has no computer available in prison) and the material just keeps on coming.

See more at:

http://www.ozarkmt.com/authors/james-nussbaumer

Books by James Nussbaumer

The Master of Everything
Published by: Ozark Mountain Publishing

Mastering Your Own Spiritual Freedom
Published by: Ozark Mountain Publishing

For more information about any of the above titles, soon to be released titles, or other items in our catalog, write, phone or visit our website:

Ozark Mountain Publishing, Inc.
PO Box 754, Huntsville, AR 72740
479-738-2348/800-935-0045
www.ozarkmt.com

If you liked this book, you might also like:

Don't Change the Channel
by Blair Styra

Sit A Bit
by Victor Parachin

Raising Our Vibrations
by Sherri Cortland

Feng Shui From the Inside, Out
by Victoria Pendragon

We Are the Creators
by Lee Sumpter

Embracing the Human Journey
by Janie Wells

A New Earth Rising
by Charmian Redwood

For more information about any of the above titles, soon to be released titles, or other items in our catalog, write, phone or visit our website:

Ozark Mountain Publishing, Inc.
PO Box 754, Huntsville, AR 72740
479-738-2348
www.ozarkmt.com

Other Books By Ozark Mountain Publishing, Inc.

Dolores Cannon
A Soul Remembers Hiroshima
Between Death and Life
Conversations with Nostradamus,
    Volume I, II, III
The Convoluted Universe -Book One,
    Two, Three, Four, Five
The Custodians
Five Lives Remembered
Jesus and the Essenes
Keepers of the Garden
Legacy from the Stars
The Legend of Starcrash
The Search for Hidden Sacred Knowledge
They Walked with Jesus
The Three Waves of Volunteers and the
    New Earth
Aron Abrahamsen
Holiday in Heaven
Out of the Archives – Earth Changes
Justine Alessi & M. E. McMillan
Rebirth of the Oracle
Kathryn/Patrick Andries
Naked In Public
Kathryn Andries
The Big Desire
Dream Doctor
Soul Choices: Six Paths to Find Your Life
    Purpose
Soul Choices: Six Paths to Fulfilling
    Relationships
Patrick Andries
Owners Manual for the Mind
Tom Arbino
You Were Destined to be Together
Rev. Keith Bender
The Despiritualized Church
Dan Bird
Waking Up in the Spiritual Age
O.T. Bonnett, M.D./Greg Satre
Reincarnation: The View from Eternity
What I Learned After Medical School
Why Healing Happens
Julia Cannon
Soul Speak – The Language of Your Body
Ronald Chapman
Seeing True
Albert Cheung
The Emperor's Stargate
Jack Churchward
Lifting the Veil on the Lost Continent of Mu
The Stone Tablets of Mu
Sherri Cortland
Guide Group Fridays
Raising Our Vibrations for the New Age
Spiritual Tool Box
Windows of Opportunity

Cinnamon Crow
Chakra Zodiac Healing Oracle
Teen Oracle
Michael Dennis
Morning Coffee with God
God's Many Mansions
Claire Doyle Beland
Luck Doesn't Happen by Chance
Jodi Felice
The Enchanted Garden
Max Flindt/Otto Binder
Mankind: Children of the Stars
Arun & Sunanda Gandhi
The Forgotten Woman
Maiya & Geoff Gray-Cobb
Angels -The Guardians of Your Destiny
Seeds of the Soul
Carolyn Greer Daly
Opening to Fullness of Spirit
Julia Hanson
Awakening To Your Creation
Donald L. Hicks
The Divinity Factor
Anita Holmes
Twidders
Antoinette Lee Howard
Journey Through Fear
Vara Humphreys
The Science of Knowledge
Victoria Hunt
Kiss the Wind
James H. Kent
Past Life Memories As A Confederate
    Soldier
Mandeep Khera
Why?
Dorothy Leon
Is Jehovah An E.T
Mary Letorney
Discover The Universe Within You
Sture Lönnerstrand
I Have Lived Before
Irene Lucas
Thirty Miracles in Thirty Days
Susan Mack & Natalia Krawetz
My Teachers Wear Fur Coats
Patrick McNamara
Beauty and the Priest
Maureen McGill
Baby It's You
Maureen McGill & Nola Davis
Live From the Other Side
Henry Michaelson
And Jesus Said – A Conversation
Dennis Milner
Kosmos

Other Books By Ozark Mountain Publishing, Inc.

Guy Needler
Avoiding Karma
Beyond the Source – Book 1, Book 2
The History of God
The Origin Speaks
James Nussbaumer
The Master of Everything
Mastering Your own Spiritual Freedom
Sherry O'Brian
Peaks and Valleys
Riet Okken
The Liberating Power of Emotions
John Panella
The Gnostic Papers
Victor Parachin
Sit a Bit
Nikki Pattillo
A Spiritual Evolution
Children of the Stars
Rev. Grant H. Pealer
A Funny Thing Happened on the
    Way to Heaven
Worlds Beyond Death
Karen Peebles
The Other Side of Suicide
Victoria Pendragon
Born Healers
Feng Shui from the Inside, Out
Sleep Magic
Michael Perlin
Fantastic Adventures in Metaphysics
Walter Pullen
Evolution of the Spirit
Christine Ramos, RN
A Journey Into Being
Debra Rayburn
Let's Get Natural With Herbs
Charmian Redwood
A New Earth Rising
Coming Home to Lemuria
David Rivinus
Always Dreaming

Briceida Ryan
The Ultimate Dictionary of Dream
    Language
M. Don Schorn
Elder Gods of Antiquity
Legacy of the Elder Gods
Gardens of the Elder Gods
Reincarnation...Stepping Stones of Life
Garnet Schulhauser
Dance of Heavenly Bliss
Dancing Forever with Spirit
Dancing on a Stamp
Annie Stillwater Gray
Education of a Guardian Angel
The Dawn Book
Blair Styra
Don't Change the Channel
Natalie Sudman
Application of Impossible Things
L.R. Sumpter
We Are the Creators
Dee Wallace/Jarrad Hewett
The Big E
Dee Wallace
Conscious Creation
James Wawro
Ask Your Inner Voice
Janie Wells
Embracing the Human Journey
Payment for Passage
Dennis Wheatley/ Maria Wheatley
The Essential Dowsing Guide
Jacquelyn Wiersma
The Zodiac Recipe
Sherry Wilde
The Forgotten Promise
Stuart Wilson & Joanna Prentis
Atlantis and the New Consciousness
Beyond Limitations
The Essenes -Children of the Light
The Magdalene Version
Power of the Magdalene
Robert Winterhalter
The Healing Christ

For more information about any of the above titles, soon to be released titles,
or other items in our catalog, write, phone or visit our website:
PO Box 754, Huntsville, AR 72740
479-738-2348/800-935-0045
www.ozarkmt.com

For more information about any of the titles published by Ozark Mountain Publishing, Inc., soon to be released titles, or other items in our catalog, write, phone or visit our website:

Ozark Mountain Publishing, Inc.

PO Box 754

Huntsville, AR 72740

479-738-2348/800-935-0045

www.ozarkmt.com